Early praise for Pulse of Perseverance

Pulse of Perseverance is the honest, deeply personal tale of three young black men's refusal to succumb to failure and how, together, they overcame daunting odds to take their place among the just five percent of U.S. doctors who are black. Through writing as passionate as it is relatable, the authors provide an unflinching look at the barriers black Americans face as they try to move out of the place society has designated for them. This book is a searing indictment of our still separate and unequal education system, one that ensures the road to becoming a doctor, or a lawyer or professor, will be much harder for black children than it will be for white.

Yet, at its core, *Pulse of Perseverance* is an inspirational story of what can be accomplished with dedication, the support of people with similar goals, and the investment from institutions dedicated to black success. This book is the North Star for every black child who sees something greater for himself than the world would have him believe.

--Nikole Hannah-Jones, Staff Writer, The New York Times Magazine

Pulse of Perseverance

THREE BLACK DOCTORS ON THEIR JOURNEY TO SUCCESS

Book I: Pierre Johnson MD
Book II: Maxime Madhere MD
Book III: Joseph Semien Jr MD

First Printing: 2017
ISBN: 099927970X
ISBN-13: 9780999279700
Library of Congress Control Number: 2017918247
Uplifting Visions, Country Club Hills, IL

Disclaimer: Some names and identifying details have been changed to protect the privacy of individuals
Published by Uplifting Visions (via CreateSpace)
Country Club Hills, IL 60478
Editing by Erika DeSimone
www.thepulseofp3.com

This book could not have been accomplished without all of the people who poured their hearts, energy, wisdom, time, and knowledge into our lives. None of us could have reached this level of success without you. We also acknowledge that part of our duty is to pay all of these blessings forward. That is why we have dedicated our lives to working each day towards building a more equitable society. Pulse of Perseverance is the first step.

Contents

Preface

By Maxime Madhere, Pierre Johnson, and Joseph Semien Jr.

AMERICA IS, AND ALWAYS HAS been, a country divided along racial lines, despite our Founding Fathers' declaration that all men are created equal. Over two hundred and forty years after the founding of this nation, black communities still face inequities across the board, and nowhere is this more true than in America's urban and inner-city neighborhoods. Substandard schools, violence in the community, income disparity, drugs, crime, absentee parents, and a legal system where, as President Obama stated in 2015, "African Americans are more likely to be arrested; they are more likely to be sentenced to more time for the same crime,"[1] all create an environment where achieving academic and professional success is a challenge. This means that for many African American children, whatever innate spark of curiosity, wonder, talent, or ambition they possess is very often extinguished at an early age. The media do little to help. In this hyperconnected, 24/7-news world, features and programming highlighting the strengths of black communities and the achievements of black professionals are still largely absent from our screens.

Young black men in particular face yet another barrier to success. Society as a whole "expects" insultingly little from us. We are perpetually considered uneducated, disinterested academically, unambitious in our goals, neglectful of

---

1 For supporting information, visit the archives of the Executive Office of the President of the United States at https://obamawhitehouse.archives.gov/blog/2015/07/15/president-obama-our-criminal-justice-system-isnt-smart-it-should-be.

our children, and unengaged in our communities. We face a whole host of these and other, even crueler biases every day, biases that attempt to define us by the color of our skin and inhibit what we can accomplish as individuals, professionals, fathers, citizens, and role models.

Pulse of Perseverance is the story of three black men on the road to success. By its very existence, our story counters the racist narratives that remain so deeply embedded in our society. All three of us came from modest, urban backgrounds, yet each of us is today a board-certified doctor. Just like anyone else, we made our fair share of mistakes along the way, but we never wavered in our desire to practice medicine, and we never gave up in the face of adversity. No media message ever tainted our ambition; no disadvantage ever prevented us from achieving our goals.

When the three of us first met at Xavier University of Louisiana, we thought it was merely a coincidence. Yet, now we understand that our meeting was no mere happenstance but rather designed by God Himself. In the fall of 1998, all three of us were struggling premed students. Each of us was smart and determined, but adjusting to the premed curriculum was one of the hardest transitions any of us had faced. We were each learning that hard work was not the only ingredient needed for success. What we needed was brotherhood.

When we met, the bond we formed was instantaneous, unlike anything we had ever experienced before. At the core of each of our souls was a fiery determination to achieve despite the odds—our will to succeed was just as important as our will to breathe. God planted a seed into each of our souls. We needed the strength from one another to cultivate those seeds. The support, direction, strength, and guidance we gave to one another linked us together in brotherhood.

Our bond carried through our premed college years and medical school, then grew as we moved into our residencies and private practices. We have now teamed up to create *Pulse* not just to share our stories and provide inspiration, but also to highlight an alarming trend in the medical field: in 2014, there were fewer black men matriculating from medical schools (515) than there were in 1978 (542).[2] We believe that chief among the reasons for this abysmal statistic

2 For supporting data, visit the Association of American Medical Colleges website at https://members.aamc.org/eweb/upload/Altering%20the%20Course%20-%20Black%20Males%20in%20Medicine%20AAMC.pdf.

is that young black men lack real-life, relatable models of success. After all, how can even the brightest young man of color be expected to pursue an MD when society at large tells him that he isn't welcome in this profession? We hope that our words encourage many more young men and women of African descent to explore high-level careers in the medical field.

To our readers who are considering, or who perhaps have already embarked on the path to medicine, we want you to know that, yes, we understand what you are going through, and we do know where you're coming from. None of us was expected to succeed, yet today, we have all achieved our dreams. It will be no different for you: achievement is yours to earn. No matter the challenges you face, no matter how overwhelmed or lonely you may feel at times, you will succeed with hard work, dedication, commitment, and God's guiding light—no one can ever take these precious gifts from you. Always remember that your life, your future, and your freedom are priceless.

BOOK I

Pierre's Story

Foreword

My motivation for sharing my story is that I know there is an underprivileged kid out there somewhere who needs to hear it. One of the biggest problems I see today is that too many of our children grow up in impoverished neighborhoods and are forced to attend dilapidated, underresourced schools without textbooks and sit in classrooms with teachers who are not prepared to teach them. This sends these children a clear message about how little we as a society value their education, and too many of our children cannot help but internalize this. These same children then look around their communities and often see few black professionals and instead look to popular culture for examples of success. What this means is that for black children in particular, rappers and athletes not only define "success," but they define "black success." The media bombards us with these messages while images of black doctors, lawyers, engineers, and other professionals are nowhere to be seen. We are a minority within the minority of professionals. Our success goes unnoticed, and our stories remain untold.

Yet I know that there's a child out there from the South Side of Chicago or somewhere similar who wants to be a doctor or lawyer but who doesn't see even the faintest path to achievement. A child who society says has no chance of professional success. A child who has never seen a doctor or lawyer who looks like him or her and who believes professional goals are only far-fetched dreams.

I have found my own path to success as a physician, and I impact the lives of my patients and their families on a daily basis. Today I teach my own children never to take success for granted—success takes hard work and dedication; it's not something that's inherited. Perhaps sharing my testimony is also a part of my purpose: if I can reach even one kid struggling to find a path toward his or her own professional goals, my mission will be accomplished.

CHAPTER 1

Chi-Town Raised Me

I WAS THREE YEARS OLD. My mother and I were running frantically down the street. I remember exactly where we were because we ran past my preschool. We were running from my father, who was high out of his mind, with a disheveled appearance in jeans and a sleeveless undershirt.

"Why are we running from Daddy?" I cried to my mother, confused and scared. I remember the look of utter terror, panic, and confusion on my mom's face as she answered, "We're just going to Grandma's." We were jogging, as I remember looking back and seeing my father speed walking behind us. Cars were driving by, but no one stopped to offer assistance. From the outside looking in, it likely appeared to be a mother with her child, trying to rush to get somewhere. Besides, people typically do not involve themselves in domestic quarrels where I'm from.

We sought refuge at my paternal grandparents' house, which was about a half a mile away from our apartment on Eighty-Third Street. By the time we arrived, we had managed to put two or three blocks between us and my father. My grandmother let us in, and my mom took me straight to the bedroom. We crawled under the covers; I thought for a moment that we were safe. A few minutes later, my father came into the bedroom, dragged my mom into the hallway by her ankle, and beat her.

Looking back, from a crisis standpoint, it would have made more sense if we had fled to my maternal grandparents' house—we actually passed their home on the way to my father's people. But my mother, even when her own safety is threatened, has always put others first. I think she suspected that her father would have shot my father in order to protect us.

To call my childhood dysfunctional would be an understatement. Both of my parents were addicted to drugs. They tried to conceal it, but I can remember plates of cocaine hidden under beds, crack pipes, and shoeboxes full of marijuana and drug paraphernalia. Our kitchen door was a swinging door. There was always a sliver I could peek through undetected, and I often saw my parents using drugs. In an effort to get them to stop, I'd knock on the door and ask for something to eat or drink. My ploy never worked.

My father worked for General Motors, at a job that his father had gotten for him. In fact, my grandfather's reputation at the company was the only reason my father was able to keep that job at all—time and time again, my father would fail his drug test, and time and time again, my grandfather put his name on the line to get my father another chance. More often than not, it became my job to provide clean urine for my father; my mother would wake me out of my sleep in the middle of the night to fill his testing cups. As a very young child, I was proud of myself for doing a "great deed" to help my father—I had no idea I was helping him to pass his drug tests. By the time I was just a few years older, I realized what I was doing, and I resented it deeply.

Drugs affect people in many different ways. I learned this in my own home at a very early age. When my mother was high, she was very functional. Outside of the classic "glassy-eyed" appearance of drug users, she looked like she usually did; she acted normally and answered questions appropriately. However, my father was quite different. I could tell he was high just by looking at him—he would sweat profusely, his eyes would bulge, and his lips would become chalky and dry.

Far worse than that were the mental effects of his drug use. When he was high, my father became delusional. He'd turn over tables, rummage through closets, and ransack the entire house looking for "clues" to "prove" my mother was cheating on him. These rages would sometimes last for hours on end. When he couldn't find evidence of the conspiracy, my father would turn physical and beat my mother. I watched as this cycle played out over and over again.

For whatever reason, my father never got physically violent with me. I guess I can be thankful for that because being physically abused would have made my story very different—I probably would have focused on myself rather than on my mother. During these many years of physical and emotional anguish, my mom developed a twisted kind of comfort from dysfunction, and I developed a deep empathy for her. I learned as a young boy that one of my purposes in life was to help others who could not help themselves.

It is my firm belief that every boy needs a strong man in his life in order to become a man himself. For a young boy, love and guidance from a male figure are paramount. However, that man doesn't have to be a boy's biological father. A father figure can teach a young boy valuable lessons through meaningful interactions, even when that father figure can't be present every day. For me, my father's drug abuse—and later, his abandonment—meant that there was a void in my life.

I am truly blessed that my maternal grandfather, Otis Johnson, completely filled that void for me in my early life and taught me about being a true man. Although I did spend a lot of day-to-day time with my grandfather, the lessons he imparted could have been achieved even if we weren't physically close. He taught me how to fish, play baseball, and run on the balls of my feet. These are all fond memories that I have of this extraordinary man, but what truly shaped me was my grandfather's generosity. He loved to garden and would sell his produce locally, but he would also give food away to the homeless and to others in need. Although he taught me the value of a dollar and how to save and spend money wisely, he would also give without reservation: each and every time a person asked for change on the street, my grandfather would give whatever coins he had in his pocket. He was a model of charity and selflessness. Without my grandfather to impart these crucial values to me, I don't know who I would be today. My grandfather's influence is one of the biggest reasons why I now value mentoring and dedicate my time to reaching out to youth.

My maternal grandmother, Eva Johnson, was my favorite person in the world. I adored her with all the reverence and enthusiasm that a kid could have. She took me everywhere with her, including to her salon, where she worked as a beautician; I think I spent more time with her than anyone else. She was my oasis from my turbulent home, and she made me feel special, appreciated, and deeply loved. My grandmother's friends would foster my sense of self as well: one of her clients used to call me "The President," and she told me every week that I would be president someday. If this seems like a small thing, it's not: these words helped plant the seed of achievement in me. My grandmother enveloped me in her world and gave me a safe space. There's really no way to qualify her influence on my life; without her as a constant, I don't know if I would've learned to believe in myself so strongly.

My aunt Aileen, my mother's twin sister, had a huge impact on my childhood. As my godmother, she was never apprehensive about challenging me. When I was five or six years old, she asked me what I wanted to be when I grew up. This might sound like a trivial, standard question, but her insistence on a realistic answer made this one of the defining moments of my life.

My young self knew the answer to her question: I was going to be a pro basketball player! However, my aunt didn't accept this, nor did she accept my alternate answer of being a pro baseball player. Perhaps most adults, afraid of discouraging a young child's dreams, would've stopped there, but Aunt Aileen demanded a "plan B." More importantly, she didn't stop asking until I had an answer.

It took me several days, but finally, I found my "plan B" on *The Cosby Show.* I was impressed by the character of Heathcliff Huxtable, who was both a doctor and an example of a strong father. Dr. Huxtable was my first exposure to a professional black male in a position of authority. Thus, my "plan B" emerged: I would become a doctor. By setting a goal for myself, I was able to link short-term goals, like doing well in school, to a greater, long-term journey. My main dream of playing pro basketball would remain for many, many years to come, but certainly, my aunt had fundamentally altered my worldview: I learned to think about myself and the paths my life could take in new ways.

My mother had wanted to go to college, but my father convinced her to forgo her education and stay with him instead; she didn't want the same for me. This is why, despite her addiction, my mother fostered learning in the home from the time I was old enough to hold a crayon. Even before I started preschool, she bought me Scholastic workbooks from the grocery store; she would sit with me, and we'd work through them together. These were some of my favorite moments because they showed my mother's true nature, which is deeply nurturing and loving. She enrolled me in the Chatham Preschool when I was three years old, and I was reading before I started kindergarten. Throughout my childhood, in my mother's house, there was no playtime without some form of schoolwork required first.

My father's sister Karen was a fifth-grade teacher at Saint Sabina Academy, which I attended from kindergarten until fourth grade. To this day, Saint Sabina is run by the well-known social activist Father Michael Pfleger. The school's mission is derived from Proverbs 22:6: *Train a child in the way he should go, and when he is old he will not turn from it.* This is exactly what Saint Sabina Academy accomplished with me, for the school instilled in me a solid basis for my education. I've carried this foundation with me throughout my entire life.

Saint Sabina was also my first real exposure to religion; in fact, the centerpiece mural at S. Sabina Church—a vibrant painting of Jesus in the hands of God—affected my young mind so profoundly that the image is now tattooed on my back. My personal trust in God would form strongly in my preteen years, but my spiritual maturity stems from my time in Father Pfleger's school.

I took school very seriously. I wanted to have the best grades and be the smartest kid! I have always had an extremely competitive spirit; it's a defining characteristic of my personality. Although some people would look at this as a negative trait, I view it as a blessing. There is no way that I would have ever dreamed of becoming a physician, let alone achieved that dream, without my strong desire to win.

As early as first grade, I kept every graded assignment and all of my homework in folders that I organized by subject; by fifth grade, I had developed a full Trapper Keeper system. With my aunt's support, I took pride in every assignment I completed. I was never intimidated by another student's intellect; I competed with every classmate because, in my mind, I felt that I was the smartest. Throughout elementary school, my hunger to be the best fueled me, and I would go to great lengths to prove myself. Whenever I disputed a grade, I was always prepared to present all of my graded work to prove that the given grade was incorrect. I worked hard and always made the honor roll.

CHAPTER 2

The Fascination of Life

When I was nine years old, my mother became pregnant with my brother Elliot. This was fascinating! I wanted to know everything about pregnancy, everything about a developing fetus. As I watched my mother's belly grow, my curiosity grew too. Even after my mother answered my initial questions about pregnancy, I continued to ask increasingly complex questions: How did this living being start from two people having sex? How will this new person grow inside of my mother and survive? What was childbirth like? Every answer led to more questions. My curiosity about pregnancy could not be satiated, and I was searching for guidance.

I am a firm believer that everything in life happens for a reason. My mother's Obstetrician, Dr. Patterson, was a middle-aged black man who had his own private practice on the South Side of Chicago. His demeanor was similar to mine, in that he was very down to earth. When I came into the office with my mom, he would talk to me as if I were his own son and ask me about school. He would also let me know how rough the road ahead would be and how I needed to remain focused and work as hard as I possibly could. He taught me to always keep my mind steadfast on my goals and never let anyone deter me from them. I remember going to prenatal appointments, and Dr. Patterson allowed me to help find my brother's heartbeat. It's the small things like this that impact kids the most. Dr. Patterson went well beyond standard prenatal care for my mother; he was a compassionate professional who saw the importance of talking to a young boy whose curiosity was alight with a million questions. Every time my mother took me to her appointments, Dr. Patterson would find time to talk with me. He'd show me charts and models, and he would answer whatever pressing questions were in my nine-year-old head. Until I met Dr. Patterson, the only other black doctors I'd ever seen were on TV. I marveled at this black doctor and his day-to-day life of taking care of his patients and family. Dr. Patterson was tangible proof that the dream I witnessed on TV could be achieved for someone who looked like me.

The age of nine marked a bittersweet time for me. I was ecstatic about Elliot's birth, and I embraced the role of being a big brother—I wanted to teach him everything. At the same time, my parents' addictions were consuming the family, and that year brought the tumultuous end to their highly toxic and dysfunctional relationship.

By this time, we were living in a modest house my paternal grandfather had bought on Eighty-Sixth and Calumet Avenue, right across the street from his own home. We had moved there a few years earlier because my father had grown increasingly dependent on his own father, who enabled my father's complete lack of responsibility. Both of my paternal grandparents blamed my mother for my father's poor choices in life, even though nothing could have been further from the truth.

Some of my fondest childhood memories occurred in this home, but this house also hosted some of my worst memories as well. Having a new baby in the home brought on new stresses, and for my parents, stress equated to heavier drug use—it was their only coping mechanism. This meant that my father went into his rages all the more often and was that much more violent toward my mother.

By this time, I had already grown to hate my father for beating my mother and—in my mind—nine years old was plenty old enough to start defending her. One night, I'd simply had enough: I could not stand by and watch as he pinned my mother against the refrigerator and began choking her. I reached back and punched my father in his side with as much might as a scrawny kid like me possibly could. I got my father's attention—he immediately stopped choking my mom and stared at me with a look of utter dismay and disbelief. In that moment, my hatred for my father grew to new heights. At this point, I was old enough not to be scared anymore, but I was angry at the dysfunction. I had seen far too many instances of drug-induced beatings. I couldn't stand to sit back and watch it anymore. During these episodes, my mother turned into a shell of herself, and I resented my father for what he was putting us through. I was fortunate that night because my father certainly could have hurt me gravely or perhaps even killed me, but God protected me, as always.

Days later, when my father was sober, he scolded me for punching him. No apologies, no remorse. He threatened to hurt me if I ever did something like that again. My reply was simple, "Then don't ever hit my mother again."

I never had to experience my father abusing my mother again, but not because my father reformed in any way. Rather, it was because General Motors forced him to relocate. He moved to Baltimore and left me, my mother, and my brother behind.

My father's desertion was the beginning of my mother's slide to rock bottom. Drugs were her only means of coping with the depression of abandonment and the stress of now having to care for her two children as a single parent. She began using more and more heavily as our circumstances grew more difficult. Because my paternal grandfather owned our house, he of course put us out not too long after my father left. We moved to a small one-bedroom apartment on Eighty-First and Maryland. Within a few months, my family life was so unstable that my mother sent me to live with my Aunt Aileen during the academic year. Her home in Glenwood was only about twenty miles away, but it was a whole new world.

CHAPTER 3

A Taste of Stability

LIVING IN GLENWOOD PROVIDED MY first sense of stability. My aunt and uncle had been married for seven years; their daughter Nefetari is six years older than I am. Even though Nefetari is technically my aunt's stepdaughter, Nefetari accepted me as her little brother, and we have remained close over the years. The four of us lived in a three-bedroom, two-bathroom home with our dog, Spencer. Moving into my aunt's house was truly a blessing for me—one that wouldn't have been bestowed if my early years were not so dysfunctional. I truly believe that this move was part of God's master plan for me, even though I couldn't understand that at the time.

My uncle Sterling offered me an example of how a man should provide for and protect his family. He had a steady job as a high school gym teacher in Chicago. He had played collegiate basketball at Tuskegee University, and he often worked with me to improve my game. I considered him my father during this time. Ultimately, though, his marriage to my aunt ended in divorce a few years after I moved back to Chicago.

Glenwood was the beginning of my personal relationship with God. In Chicago, we rarely attended church; in Glenwood, the four of us went to church every Sunday. I can't say that I liked going to church as a ten-year-old, but I did recognize the importance of prayer. I drew comfort from talking with God, and I could clearly hear His message to me. He told me I would succeed, no matter what came, as long as I welcomed Him into my life. His presence became so profound that I quickly understood, with surprising clarity, the path my life would take.

Glenwood wasn't always easy for me. I suppose some people would assume that the suburbs must have seemed like heaven to me, but I was away from my mother for the first time, and Chicago was my home—and no matter where you're from, home is home. Initially, I experienced a sort of culture shock: I went from an inner-city, all-black school mere blocks away from gangbangers and addicts to playing with white kids and attending bar mitzvahs. This was my first real exposure to diversity, which would later help immensely in my schooling. However, Glenwood was also my first identifiable exposure to racism. I had been taught about the Civil Rights Movement by my grandparents, but I had never felt racism in my everyday life until I moved out of Chicago. I couldn't understand why people hated me without knowing me.

Some of this racism was latent, but some was more explicit. I remember being chased home one afternoon by a friend's racist neighbor for the "crime" of playing basketball while black. Later on, as I became interested in girls, I learned of the racist taboos against interracial dating. Merely having a crush on a white girl brought taunts of "jungle fever" from my friends, at a time when I was especially sensitive to, and fearful of, ridicule—as most preteens are.

Even though these experiences were hurtful, facing racism prepared me for a future in which I would always face challenges because of the color of my skin. There would be times in my life when, as a black male, I'd be completely isolated from my peers. There would be moments in my professional training when bias and prejudice would threaten my entire career.

I attended Brookwood from fifth through eighth grade. My education in Glenwood's middle-class environment was excellent, and these experiences were unequivocally essential for my success. Brookwood was the first time I experienced real intellectual competition. In Chicago, I was always one of the smartest kids in my class, but in Brookwood, I was treated like an average student, challenged by kids who were smarter than me, and expected to prove myself academically.

When I was first enrolled, I was not placed in any honors classes. I took this as an insult. Exclusion from the "gifted" kids lit a fire in my competitive spirit. Even at ten years old, I knew that many thought a kid from the South Side of

Chicago with drug-addicted parents shouldn't even be mentioned in the same educational breath as kids whose parents were professionals. But I didn't care what they thought about me, and their perceptions only drove me to study harder: I double-checked each homework assignment, made good use of my Trapper Keepers, and studied hard for all tests and quizzes. The tools that I learned in these four short years would later prove to be my lifeline during the hurricane I experienced in college and the tsunami that was medical school, especially since my high school years would fail me academically.

By the time I was in eighth grade, I had established myself as one of the smartest kids in the school, but to me, being "one of" the smartest kids wasn't good enough. It wasn't enough for me to be the smartest black kid—I didn't accept that consolation prize. I wanted to be the best! Challenging myself to outperform my counterparts of other races and ethnicities pushed me to be the best that I could be. Eventually, I grew to understand that the only person I needed to compete with was myself. The "regular me" would always be good enough to make decent grades; the "best me" would shine more brightly than anyone would ever suspect.

While my home life during the school year in Glenwood was stable, any feelings of pride that I gained from my scholastic achievements were completely humbled by my summers in Chicago. During the summers, the stability of the school year was entirely stripped away. In this sense, living between these two worlds made the best years of my life the worst years of my life as well.

Our family was growing rapidly. Within my four Glenwood years, my mom, whose drug addiction was still raging, had three more children. When I was eleven, my sister Camille was born after one of my father's few visits home. My half brother Kyle was born the next year. His father, Rod, was a South Side contractor with a family of his own. He turned his back on my mother and Kyle, refusing to spend time with my brother or support him financially. (I later confronted this man as an adult; he hid behind his wife and refused to meet his own son.) Two years later, when I was fourteen, my youngest sibling, Tyler, was born; I never met his father. Because I was very mature and responsible, it was natural for me to become a father figure to my siblings, even though it was far more responsibility than any young kid should have had.

These summers were very hard, even though I do have fond memories of spending time with my mom and siblings. My mother knew her addiction had a huge impact on our family, but she was never able to quit, despite her desire to put drug abuse behind her. She was unemployed, and public assistance was barely enough to pay the rent—let alone the utilities—and drugs further impeded her ability to provide for us financially. She should have had support from my father, or from the fathers of Kyle and Tyler, but all three men abandoned her.

My mother loved us deeply and was always very nurturing, but before she knew it, we were in a vicious poverty cycle. There were periods when our electricity was turned off, and we had to use candles to see at night. There were moments when we didn't have gas; we heated water in the microwave in order to bathe. We were evicted from at least two apartments. I recall our family's belongings being put out on the street as we were evicted; my mother had to scramble to borrow money from friends and family to raise the rent by the end of the day. One of the most embarrassing and humbling moments of my life occurred during our second eviction: I was literally sitting on our sofa on our front lawn, in full view of the street, as our stuff was carried outside. Again, my mother had to borrow money from friends and family to pay rent by the end of the day. Food stamps kept food on the table, which was one of the very few certainties of our lives. In that regard, I have always been thankful. I knew kids who were in a perpetual state of hunger; if nothing else, my mom always made sure that we were fed.

My mother finally reached her lowest point in 1994. Things had become so unstable at home, and her addiction had grown so severe, that she felt she had no choice but to put Tyler up for adoption. My mother's true nature is very loving. It's not that she didn't want to care for us in every way possible; it's that she couldn't—not with addiction controlling her life. However, placing Tyler up for adoption was her ultimate wake-up call; the loss of him as a part of our family proved to be the one thing that could burn through the hold drugs had on her. The family Tyler was placed with was extremely religious and upstanding; they renamed him Enoch when they took guardianship, and my brother probably would've had a positive experience growing up in their home. But a positive experience is not the same as a family; there would have forever been a void in Tyler's life, as well as in ours.

It wasn't until this point that my mother took a step back and reflected on her life. She knew the only way to get Tyler back was to find the help she needed. She entered a one-month inpatient rehab program. There she learned the tools and techniques to keep herself clean and—possibly for the first time in her life—had the time and space to focus on herself. We went to live with my aunt, and so I spent that time, which was the last month of my eighth-grade summer vacation, caring for Elliot, Camille, and Kyle, who were five, three, and two years old, respectively.

My mother's addiction and ultimate triumph were necessary pieces of the puzzle on the road to my success. Being a father figure to my siblings taught me a sense of responsibility that I wouldn't have received at any other juncture in my life. This sense of responsibility has made me a better student, better father, better doctor, and overall, a better man.

I am proud to say that after rehab, my mother never touched drugs again. My mother's triumph is the most inspirational accomplishment I've ever witnessed. I couldn't be more proud of her; she's a truly phenomenal human being. She returned home with a new focus and—just as importantly—a passionate desire to keep that focus. Tyler soon came home for good; our family was complete.

Looking at my mother today, you'd never suspect the hardships she survived. Decades later, she's still 100 percent drug-free and has had a job in health insurance for almost twenty years. She'd give the shirt off her back to a stranger in need. She's an exceptional grandmother and the pillar of our family. She's always been my biggest supporter; there is no "me" without my mom.

With Tyler now home, my mother wanted nothing more than to provide for us and offer us stability. The problem was, she'd lost everything before getting clean; she had to start from the bottom. By starting from the bottom, I mean she had no job and no place for us to live. By this time, my maternal grandparents had separated, and the only place we could turn to for shelter was my grandmother's one-bedroom apartment. Six people, four of them children, under one tiny roof.

CHAPTER 4

Wild Hundreds

IN THE FALL OF 1994, I returned to Glenwood. I was planning on living with my aunt and uncle during the week and returning to Chicago for as many weekends as possible to help my mother. I was entering ninth grade that year and was supposed to attend Marion Catholic High School, but when my uncle took me to my first day of school, the administration told us flatly and absolutely that I wouldn't be able to attend because I had registered too late. I've always wondered if Marion would have been willing to bend the rules if my skin looked more like the majority of the school's student body.

The only available public school option in Glenwood was the local high school, which didn't appeal to me. By this time, sports were undeniably my number one priority, so I wanted a school with an excellent athletic program. When Marion Catholic didn't work out, I felt I had no choice but to go back to Chicago. This was a moment in my life where I should have had a father to help me make the decision that was best for my future, but I was left to make the choice on my own. I knew I would continue to maintain my good grades no matter what high school I went to, but I gave absolutely no thought to the *quality* of my education.

I was familiar with Saint Martin de Porres High School, which was roughly one mile from my grandmother's apartment on 111th and King Drive, because the grandfather of one of my teammates had taken us for practice sessions with the school's head coach, Mike Manderino. In 1994, Saint Martin's team had won the Catholic League basketball title and had competed in a Class A state tournament. That was all I needed to know; I chose my school.

Unlike at Marion, my late registration at Saint Martin was met with acceptance instead of intolerance. The very first person I met at Saint Martin was a kid named Booker, who was in the office registering late, just like me. My aunt struck up a conversation with Booker's grandmother, and Booker and I started talking too. In a matter of minutes, it seemed as if we had known each other for years. We quickly learned that we both had a passion for basketball, prided ourselves on our grades, and understood that we could not get involved in gangs—as tempting as they were—if we were going to be successful.

One of the most vital pieces of advice that I can offer young kids with high ambitions is to surround themselves with like-minded people—in essence, you are the company you keep. God has always strategically placed people in my life at exactly the right moment; Booker was a constant daily reminder of what I needed to do to be successful. We kept each other in check throughout our high school years, and we made sure we never allowed each other to deviate from our chosen paths. We were friendly with other kids, of course, but we only confided in each other. Booker became more than my best friend: he is my brother.

My move back to Chicago to attend Saint Martin wasn't immediate. Initially, I commuted to Chicago with my aunt and uncle every morning, then returned to Glenwood with them in the evenings. However, once basketball started, I began training every day and soon learned that commuting wasn't going to work. I played on the freshman, junior varsity, and upperclassmen's varsity teams. All three teams had practices at different times of the day—5:30 a.m., 3:00 p.m., and 5:00 p.m. With a schedule so rigorous and demanding, I spent more and more time at my grandmother's apartment, until I completely moved in midway through my freshman year.

The living arrangements at my grandmother's were cramped, to say the least, and the experience was vastly different from my having my own bedroom in Glenwood. My grandmother slept in the apartment's only bedroom. My mom, myself, and my four siblings all slept in the ten-by-fifteen-foot living room on pallets of blankets. Eventually, Booker joined us, too, because my grandmother's apartment was much closer to our school than his house. I was content, though, because my mother was clean; this was more important to me than all else.

My mother had found work as a manager of a local Laundromat. This provided my family with some degree of financial stability, but beyond food and housing, I was on my own financially. I got a part-time job making sandwiches at Subway so that I could afford glasses, contacts, shoes, and clothes. I saved every dime that I earned for necessities; I wouldn't accept going without something just because my mother couldn't afford it. At times I was tempted to start selling marijuana so I could help my mother financially, but memories of my parents' early drug use had created in me a deep aversion to drugs, plus I was afraid of getting caught and having a criminal record.

It was at this time that God blessed me with an unusual, but lucrative, opportunity, one that eventually tied into my career as a doctor. During my freshman year, I was sitting in my math class when my teacher, George Goewey, walked in with a horrendous haircut. He suffered through plenty of ridicule that day, and of course, I participated in the teasing. Yet my competitive spirit wouldn't let me stop there: I told George that although I'd never cut hair, I was certain that I could do a better job than his barber had.

George took that statement and challenged me. The next day, he came to school with a brand-new pair of hair clippers and told me to back up my big talk by fixing his hair. I wasn't about to back away from the challenge: I took the job seriously and worked very meticulously. His finished haircut was far from perfect, but it was vastly improved. He told me to keep the clippers as a gift.

I had no idea at the time how instrumental that first haircut would prove to be. From that day forward, I worked relentlessly to improve my skills as a barber. I cut my brothers' hair every few days and offered free haircuts to anyone in school until I was skilled enough to charge. Soon, I'd developed a gentle precision, and the demand for my services began growing like wildfire. By my sophomore year, I was not only the barber for the school but for much of my neighborhood as well. Little did I know it then, but cutting hair portended my future career: I learned much later that the first surgeons were barbers.

Cutting hair did much more for me than just putting money in my pocket—it even did more than help put me through college. Cutting hair taught me I was gifted with my hands. In high school, I was unaware how vital my years of dexterity training as a barber would be to my career. Most people call obstetricians "baby catchers," but there is much more to the profession than that. I am a skilled surgeon who specializes in minimally invasive surgery. My training with my hands began with clippers and razors long before I ever touched a scalpel, and it all started right there in math class.

George Goewey gave me a gift that affected my life more deeply than words could ever explain. He saw something special in me and was the first of the three white men who were instrumental in my success. George continued to support me throughout high school—and well beyond. He's attended every single one of my graduation ceremonies and has been a source of support every step of the way. George is a lifelong friend and a member of my extended family.

I learned many lessons during my high school years, but unfortunately, almost none of them were academic. Saint Martin was so poor academically that my educational growth was severely stunted. During my freshman year, only two of my classes offered any real education—algebra with George Goewey and English with Mr. Van Dyke. Although my first year at Saint Martin did offer some structure and discipline, this quickly changed when a new principal took over. My sophomore and junior years did not resemble anything close to what an education is supposed to be like. I learned absolutely nothing in science. My teacher did not teach us, and we would pass the time playing cards. That put me at a serious disadvantage when I later started my premed major in college. Were it not for George Goewey's math classes, I might not have learned anything at all.

In addition to the substandard education, the school's discipline system plummeted after the arrival of the new principal. There were gang fights on school grounds weekly. Food fights erupted in the cafeteria on a regular basis. Saint Martin devolved into one of Chicago's many underperforming public schools.

Due to poor funding and leadership, Saint Martin closed after my junior year in 1997. My mother had led a group of determined parents in a fight to keep the school open; I remember her being interviewed on the news and crying about the school's impending closure. I wanted Saint Martin to stay open, too, but my desires were selfish: it was my senior year and my turn to be the star of the varsity basketball team.

My friend Isaac, who was the point guard on our basketball team, urged me to transfer with him to Saint Laurence High School, a predominantly white, all-male school. I had played with Saint Laurence's team over the summer, so I already knew many of the students in the basketball program. Even though I was enrolling in a school that could've provided me with the scholastic enrichment I desperately needed, I was too focused on my athletics to take advantage of the opportunity.

As one of the few black males at Saint Laurence, I didn't feel welcome. The biggest issue for me was being a high-performing shooter on a team stacked with white shooters. Isaac's skills were different from mine; as a strong point guard, he filled in one of the team's weaknesses, and so his transition was easier. However, for me, the pushback from the parents of the other seniors was tangible: I was the new kid, a black kid, and I was changing up the team's roster as well as threatening their sons' chances of winning college scholarships. I felt this was a no-win situation, and I didn't want to be subjected to any backlash, so I chose to leave the school.

The Chicago Public Schools (CPS) had listened to the cries for help from the group of parents led by my mother; CPS purchased Saint Martin and reopened it as the Southside College Preparatory Academy. In addition, the position of head basketball coach had been promised to my uncle Sterling. The opportunity to play basketball for the man who had all but introduced me to the game was enticing.

Contrary to its name, Southside College Preparatory Academy was anything but a college prep school—in fact, it was in academic shambles. George

Goewey was gone, and with him went my education in mathematics. Most of my teachers during my senior year refused to teach us; they had no lesson plans, and when I sought help, one teacher even told me that it was not his job to teach me but the books' job. The exception was my English teacher, who did enhance my writing skills and reading comprehension. I was fortunate in this regard because I desperately needed improvement in these areas. Like most other minority students in underperforming schools, I was not taught strong reading skills; like most kids around me, I had rarely picked up a book for leisure in my life. But other than improved reading and writing, I learned very little my senior year. Again, I received no real instruction in the sciences, and so I fell even further behind in this crucial area.

As I struggled to get through my senior year of high school, I felt I had made one of the biggest mistakes ever by enrolling in Southside Prep. The school never hired my uncle but instead hired a coach with minimal experience; my team finished last in our division. The only bright spot in the uneventful end of my high school basketball career was that I made six three-point shots in my last game.

I didn't care about the quality of my education because I assumed I was smart enough to just figure it out. But good grades were important to me, and I had hoped to graduate at the top of my class. I knew I needed exceptional grades to pursue my "backup" plan in medicine. My 3.67 GPA placed me as the class salutatorian, with the valedictorian spot going to Booker. I didn't graduate with my class's highest ACT score either; I had scored a twenty-two, which also placed me second in my class. Booker had scored one point higher. Yet despite having the best two ACT scores in the class, our scores were low in the overall sense, as the average ACT scores of students in affluent high schools in Chicago at the time were in the middle to high twenties.[3] In addition to a substandard high school academic education, like most inner-city minority students, I also hadn't been taught how to take standardized tests. This deficiency would prove nearly fatal to my medical career in a few years' time.

3 Visit the Memphis Teacher Residency's subsidiary website at http://www.edgap.org for more information.

CHAPTER 5

Best Decision I Ever Made

MY PATH TO MEDICINE CERTAINLY would've been a lot easier if I had gone to a high school that had properly prepared me for my journey through college and medical school. But if that were the case, my story would be completely different; I probably wouldn't be sharing it with the world.

Choosing the right college was one of the most important decisions I have ever made in my life. If I had chosen incorrectly, I'm positive I wouldn't have been able to accomplish my goals. In my junior year of high school, I had realized that I wanted to go to college as far away from Chicago as possible. I was still very focused on basketball, so I wanted a school with a strong program. Academically speaking, I knew that I needed to go to a college that would give me the best opportunity to get into medical school. When I was researching schools, one school stood out because it ranked highest in the nation in sending African Americans on to medical school. Xavier University of Louisiana immediately became my school of destiny.

I qualified for Xavier's Howard Hughes Program, a summer program that was designed to help incoming freshmen adjust to the premed curriculum and transition more easily to campus life. At the time, I thought, "I don't need this program." I assumed that I would figure college out along the way, just like I'd done with everything else in my life. I'd heard stories of college being hard, but because I hadn't been academically challenged in four years, I had a false sense of confidence. This very nearly proved to be my undoing in the fall.

Confidence in most situations is beneficial, but when there's no experience to support that confidence, it can be disastrous. This is another important example of where a father figure would have been instrumental. However, since no one in my immediate family had ever graduated from college or had any idea of what a premed curriculum entailed, I was left to rely on my own naïve, inexperienced understanding.

I was also entirely too focused on basketball. My uncle Sterling had reached out to his professional network, and I knew Xavier's coach would have an eye on me during the fall tryouts. Rather than studying, I spent the summer of 1998 improving my game and working to save money for tuition. I didn't touch a book that summer, despite having an amazing opportunity for scholastic enrichment at my fingertips. In retrospect, shirking off the Howard Hughes Program was one of the worst decisions I've ever made.

Although I spent my summer before college focused on all the wrong things, I can honestly say I was determined to do well and succeed from the moment I stepped onto Xavier's campus. I had rarely studied in the past four years, but I knew that college would require my focus and best effort. I started off by organizing folders for every subject and creating study plans. I had never received a C in my life, and I was determined not to start then.

I often refer to my first semester of college as hell on earth because, for me, that's exactly what it was. I met my roommate, Jonathan, two weeks before school started at a reception in Chicago. Jonathan had graduated from one of Chicago's premier high schools and was used to rigorous academics, plus he was incredibly goal-oriented. Studying with Jonathan was immensely helpful because it became evident very quickly that there was a vast amount of information I had never been introduced to in high school. In other words, I didn't know how much I didn't know. I was so far behind academically that everything I was exposed to as a freshman was brand-new information—I didn't have a proper knowledge base to build on. I can barely describe how lost I was initially, especially in science: I didn't even have a working knowledge of the periodic table of elements.

Sports, too, proved to be a challenge. Despite my four years of high school basketball, my body was not prepared for the rigorous grind of collegiate conditioning. The team required two daily practices—one at 5:00 a.m. and a second at 3:30 p.m.—and before we ever touched a court, there were weeks of intense weight training, pool aerobics, and timed sprints. My body was in shock for the first month; in high school, we had only focused on playing and training, not on weights and aerobics. I would wake up nightly with charley horses, and even walking to class hurt. When we finally started practicing on the court, cramps and muscle fatigue rendered me a shell of myself as a shooter.

My dreams were crumbling one month into college. I had to balance studying mountains of material that I could barely digest with the physical hell my body was going through. Additionally, because I didn't have enough loan and scholarship money to fully cover my tuition and fees, I would stay up late cutting hair to make money, which took a toll on both my studies and my training. To make matters even more complicated, my high school girlfriend informed me that she was pregnant.

By the start of the second month, school was so difficult that my clear vision of success became as cloudy as the skies during a hurricane. The thought of becoming a father, on top of all my other struggles, was too much. Unlike my own father, I wanted to be a real father to my children, yet I knew I couldn't be a good father at this point in my life. The emotional strain was intense, but my girlfriend and I mutually agreed that neither of us was prepared to be a parent; we made the decision to terminate the pregnancy. Abortion is never an easy choice, and it was one that I never thought I'd have to make.

At Xavier, one standard policy is early and frequent tests and quizzes so that educators can assess student performance early on. At the time, I thought frequent testing was designed to torture students, but I later realized that this system was an ingenious way of identifying early on those students who were having problems transitioning to college.

My poor grades accumulated very quickly. Despite my long hours of study, my test scores were not reflective of my efforts. By mid-semester, my grades were mostly Ds, although I had managed to earn one or two Cs. At this critical juncture, I had to make one of the hardest decisions of my life: I gave up my lifelong dream of playing pro basketball.

No one truly understands how hard that decision was for me. I hit a deep depression that only Jonathan knew about because he lived with me. Giving basketball up was hard enough, but doing it at a point when I was performing poorly on the court made the decision all the more gut-wrenching. For a while, I even avoided the players on the team because I was ashamed of my decision and afraid of their ridicule. I never wanted to hear the words, "I told you so."

My world was in shambles in the fall of 1998. I had always had a close relationship with God, but my first few months in college drew me even closer to His light. In high school, I had gone to church on my own every Sunday and tithed what little money I could—this seemed the least I could do for God's blessings—but at Xavier, I began spending time with God every day. Because Xavier is a Catholic institution, Mass was held daily; I didn't attend Mass (I was raised in the Baptist church), but I would use the chapel each day to pray—in fact, some days, I would go to the chapel both in between classes and after classes were done. I knew in my heart that God had my destiny planned out, and I fervently believed that He did not bring me to Xavier to fail. I knew God had bigger plans for my life: the tribulations I was facing were only a test. The harder times got, the harder I prayed.

I was able to accept the reality that I was not mentally or academically prepared for the rigors of a premed curriculum. It seemed the more I studied, the worse my grades became—this was particularly true in my biology and other premed classes. By then, I had less than two months before the semester's end to turn things around. The problem was not my work ethic, nor was it a question of my desire to do well. The problem, as I would learn later on, was that that I didn't know how to study effectively.

Effective studying is an art in itself. Without efficient and effective studying, retaining information is virtually impossible. I would spend hours in the library, but my retention level was severely deficient. I was so desperate that I even tried the "Mega Memory System" to enhance retention. I'd listen to the program's memory-enhancement tapes while curled up in my dorm room—Jonathan thought this was the funniest thing in the world. I can sit back and laugh at it now, but at the time, I felt completely helpless. All of the chips were stacked against me, and I found myself in a state of desperation. No one would've bet any money on my success at this point, not even myself.

Pressure bursts pipes, but it also makes diamonds. While many students would've quit, my "never-say-die" spirit wouldn't allow me to give up. To find strength within myself, I reflected on my life. I thought about my father's abuse, my parents' drug use, and my mother's struggle to get clean. I recalled the rage inside of me when I discovered that yet another trophy or award had been lost during our multiple evictions. I thought about the embarrassment and frustration I felt when we were thrown out of our apartments. I remembered the times when we didn't have gas or electricity. Nothing that college could throw at me could be worse than what I'd already lived through, and I was determined to ensure that my family would never have to live that way again. If I failed, I not only failed myself, but I also failed the family that was counting on me to provide a better life.

The road to medicine for a kid in my shoes is never completed alone. I thank God for introducing me to my brothers for life. I met Maxime Madhere, one of my coauthors, midway through that first semester. We'd previously had some casual conversations about music and sports, but no extensive contact. One evening, we were both leaving the library at the same time and started talking about our poor test scores. It was immediately evident that we had multiple things in common, but the most important was our shared burning desire to succeed. We learned very quickly that neither one of us would ever accept failure as an option. Max had early struggles in his life as well, but he had a more stable background from which to draw strength. Nonetheless, Max found himself in a battle during his first semester, just like I did.

After that first conversation, we committed to battling through this journey together until the end. If one of us didn't understand a concept, we wouldn't continue until we both understood it. If neither one of us was able to master a topic, we would go together to get help. We agreed to push each other to the limit, and we became a checks-and-balances system for each other.

A few weeks later, Max and I started a conversation in the library with the other coauthor of this book, Joseph Semien. It was immediately evident that Joe had the same burning desire to succeed as Max and I had. In some ways, Joe's life had been very different from mine, but in other ways, we were nearly mirrors of each other, and Joe was interested in becoming an ob-gyn, just like I was. All three of us valued success over breathing. Until I found Joe and Max, I had never met anyone else with a desire to succeed that paralleled mine; the three of us then took up the battle together. That mind-set formed the collective backbone of our brotherhood. We are brothers for life.

Xavier University itself was my saving grace. It would've been very easy for me to slip through the cracks during the academic valleys of my freshman year, but Xavier actively worked to identify and support students like me. Coming to grips with not being the smartest or most successful student was difficult, but I humbled myself and began going to the premed office every day for extra help.

I received nothing but support. Unlike at larger universities, where students are often seen as numbers, Xavier's smaller classes meant that our professors were very accessible, and they would often know students by name. Whatever advice my professors gave, I took it to heart and followed it to a tee. I took full advantage of my professors' office hours, and I joined study groups. I made it a point to verbalize my uncompromising desire to succeed—no one would doubt my commitment. Just as importantly, I was never made to feel ashamed of my deficiencies; the focus was always on making my performance stronger, never on my weaknesses.

Dr. Carmichael, the head of the premed program, certainly didn't babysit us. "I'm not going to come after you like your momma," he often said. However, he did make it clear that any student seeking help would receive it in abundance. One of the defining components of Dr. Carmichael's approach (and of Xavier as a whole) was actively discouraging academic competition among students. There were no benefits reserved for students who performed well at the expense of those who failed, and there were no classes with preconceived "expected-to-fail" quotas. Instead, the underlying assumption was that we would all pass and succeed. Every discussion was aimed at making us understand that we were a community of future doctors who all had a common goal. We were encouraged to form study groups, share information freely, and support one another. We lifted one another up, rather than shooting one another down.

I often contrast my premed orientation at Xavier with my first week at the University of Illinois College of Medicine. At Xavier, I remember sitting in a large lecture hall with other nervous freshmen; Dr. Carmichael told us that every student in the room would be a doctor if we put the work in. He told us that we were in control of our own destinies and that our goals would be achieved with hard work and sacrifice. At the University of Illinois orientation, we were told, "Look to your left, and look to your right. There's a good chance that one or both of those people will not be there at graduation." Don't get me wrong—there were plenty of students at Xavier who dropped the premed program for various reasons, but lack of support was not one of them.

Encouragement and positive reinforcement from the premed office was the breath of life that I needed after my first month of failures. Attending Xavier afforded me a priceless gift that only God knew I needed. I have been asked several times if I could have succeeded at another college without the support that Xavier provided. I honestly don't know the answer, but I can sincerely say that I am blessed by never having had the opportunity to find out.

I was recently asked about the turning point of my first semester: What was the defining moment when I knew I would succeed? Again, God works in mysterious ways. He sent me to Xavier's incredibly supportive premed program, blessed me with Max and Joe, helped me overcome the loss of basketball, and guided me through my struggles with my high school girlfriend. Yet God also sent me exactly what I needed to light a fire under my ass: one professor who was not at all encouraging when I went to him for help.

When I first went to Dr. G. at midterms for guidance that first semester, I had a D in his biology class. I told him I wanted a B by semester's end. He told me that he'd had many students with D averages at midterms but that he'd "never had one student improve to a B by the end of the semester." My initial reaction was shock and heartbreak: this man was all but telling me I would fail. I had to take a deep breath to prevent myself from getting emotional. By the time I left his office, my soul was on fire. I felt disrespected and angry; I wanted nothing more than to prove Dr. G. wrong.

Dr. G.'s reservations relit my competitive spark. I studied longer and harder, my focus intensified, and my confidence soared. I finished my first semester with an overall 3.1 GPA—and with a B in Dr. G.'s class. In fact, I had earned all Bs, plus one A. Finishing my semester with a 3.1 GPA after such a horrible start paved the way for the rest of my educational career: I now knew that there was nothing I couldn't overcome academically. I made a point to go to Dr. G.'s office after final grades to let him know he had one student who was able to accomplish what he said couldn't be done.

After completing my freshman year with such good grades, I decided that my sophomore year would be the right time to return to my dream of playing basketball. I spent that summer studying during the day—I had been accepted into the Minority Medical Education Program, a nationwide summer program—but in the evenings, I was focused on working on my game and on strenuous conditioning as well. I worked myself into prime shape and was healthier and stronger than I'd ever been.

The week I returned to New Orleans for my sophomore year, I began playing pickup games right away. But God didn't have basketball in His plans for me: I was almost literally stopped in my tracks. By the end of the week, my knees felt like they were on fire—I could barely walk. I went to the doctor and was diagnosed with jumper's knees (a type of tendonitis). Per my doctor's instructions, I rested and took anti-inflammatory medication for two weeks. Yet when I returned to the court, I couldn't get through fifteen minutes of playing without debilitating pain.

Without this injury, I would have given the lion's share of my efforts to basketball, which would have caused my grades to suffer. I wouldn't have been able to honor my pact with Max, and I would have ripped a full leg from the tripod of strength that Max, Joe, and I had formed. Perhaps I never would've made it into medical school, and who knows where I'd be today. I firmly believe God made this decision for me by putting an obstacle in my way that I physically couldn't overcome.

Since I had to accept the reality that my basketball career was over, I decided to investigate the one fraternity on campus that had caught my attention, Omega Psi Phi. I was skeptical about fraternities because the only concept I had of Greek life came from movies like Spike Lee's *School Daze*. The way I looked at it, I had resisted the temptation to join a gang in Chicago, so why in the world would I join a fraternity? Yet the brothers of Omega Psi Phi defied all my expectations, and I had told myself that if I ever changed my mind about Greek life, Omega Psi Phi would be my only choice. I had seen the "Ques" performance at the annual Bayou Classic Show during my freshman year: when they took the stage, an electricity filled the arena that I can't explain in words. The fraternity had deep religious undercurrents too—one of the founders was a Methodist bishop—and that appealed to me deeply. I also noticed a true camaraderie among the Ques that wasn't present at other fraternities. Plus, all of the fraternity brothers had a radiating bravado that commanded attention and, more importantly, respect.

Omega Psi Phi was exclusive; in fact, after my freshman year, all underclassmen members had graduated from Xavier; only two graduate students were left as members. Rather than accepting new initiates who didn't meet Omega Psi Phi's high standards, the chapter chose to stay dormant. This resonated with me, especially because I had seen other fraternities that accepted new pledges indiscriminately. To quote brother Walter Herbert Mazyck, "The value of our Fraternity is not in numbers, but in men, in real brotherhood. Eight men thoroughly immersed in the true Omega spirit are far greater assets than eighty with lukewarm enthusiasm."[4]

I pledged to Omega Psi Phi Fraternity Incorporated, Xi Sigma Chapter, in my senior year. The opportunity to bring the mystique of the fraternity back to Xavier after such a long period of dormancy was enticing, and my 3.3 GPA more than met Omega Psi Phi's academic requirements. Knowing that others had tried, but failed, to bring the fraternity back to life made pledging even more appealing.

I am so grateful for the decision I made to pledge to Omega Psi Phi in the fall of 2001. The pledge process was everything that I thought it would be multiplied by one hundred: it was hard but fair, brutal but honest. I had to prove, through recommendations letters, transcripts, and references, that I exemplified Omega's four cardinal principles: manhood, scholarship, perseverance, and uplift (community service).[5] I recited Omega poems and chants until they became a part of my heart and soul. I was pushed to my limits of tolerance and discovered that at the core of my soul is a fire that burns all the brighter in the face of adversity.

Throughout the next ten years of my life, whenever I felt tested, I would remind myself that nothing could ever be physically tougher than my pledge process. When I performed poorly on a test, I would recall the line, "But remember you are facing just what other men have met,"[6] from brother Edgar Guest's poem "See It Through." Beyond college, I have made countless bonds with Omega brothers from many chapters, which has opened doors to me that I wouldn't otherwise have had the honor of exploring.

---

4 See Omega Psi Phi's 2010 newsletter *The Oracle* at http://www.oppf.org/docs/TheOracleSummer2010.pdf for more information.

5 Visit the Omega Psi Phi website at http://www.oppf.org/member_selection.asp for more information.

6 Visit Omega Psi Phi's Auburn University chapter page at http://www.auburn.edu/student_info/greeks/omega_psi_phi/poems2.html for a partial listing of beloved Omega songs, poems, and quotes, many of which are interspersed throughout this text.

My experience at Xavier University was the most memorable four years of my life. I developed into a well-rounded student with the ability to navigate through and excel in a demanding academic environment. Although Joe, Max, and I were good students who pushed one another to the limits, we all shared a common, glaring deficiency that was never addressed specifically during our time at Xavier: skill in taking standardized tests. In my junior year, the three of us took the Medical College Admission Test (MCAT) for the first time. We all studied hard, but our standardized-test-taking deficiencies were completely exposed. We all scored poorly and faced a roadblock on our journey to our medical careers.

Standardized-test-taking skills are taught from an early age to kids from middle-class and affluent backgrounds, which is usually not the case for underprivileged minorities. In our society, there are many theories behind why there are so few minority doctors and lawyers. Theories rooted in racism hold that there is a disparity in levels of intelligence, but this couldn't be further from the truth. The disparity lies not in intelligence but in both educational quality and in test-taking skills—skills that must be taught and cultivated for years. Standardized tests are designed to measure intellect, but they are inherently flawed; these tests assume that everyone has been taught how to analyze questions appropriately and that all students receive the same quality of education. The MCAT and Law School Admission Test (LSAT) weed out more minority students than scholastic proficiency ever has. In my opinion, standardized tests are more of a reflection of test-taking skills than knowledge: those with deficient knowledge but excellent test-taking skills can perform better than knowledgeable individuals with poor test-taking skills. For example, incorrect answer options can often be weeded out by looking at a question's sentence structure, but if students aren't taught this at an early age, they will not know how to recognize these clues.

After such disappointing MCAT results, Max and I enrolled in a Kaplan review course to prepare to retake the exam. (Joe opted out of the course.) Max and I spent most evenings pouring our energy into test prep. What we learned was that effort could make up for gaps in knowledge, but it couldn't make up for a lack of test-taking skills. In our Kaplan course, we saw how students from more privileged backgrounds improved their performance on practice tests almost effortlessly, whereas Max and I put forth major efforts for marginal gains.

Although kids like me are at an obvious disadvantage, we still take the same tests to get into medical school, then take the same licensing tests and board exams later on. To expect a kid with a background like mine to narrow the educational disparity gap in only four years of college is absurd and unjust. I know this from experience; the education I received in the suburbs was vastly superior to the education I received in high school on Chicago's South Side.

I was beyond frustrated. I had no idea how to truly improve my MCAT score. I knew more studying was not the answer because subject-matter knowledge wasn't the major issue. These tests were all the harder for me because I am a very methodical thinker with a tendency to overanalyze even the smallest details. Yet standardized tests are strictly timed, and for me, this was disastrous: "speeding up" on tests went against my brain's inherent approach to analysis.

Early in my junior year, representatives from Southern Illinois University (SIU) had made a presentation about SIU's postbaccalaureate Medical/Dental Education Preparatory Program (MEDPREP) course of study. At the time of their visit, I had thought the program was likely a helpful resource but one that I wouldn't need. My MCAT score and lack of significant improvement in Kaplan taught me differently. I discussed the program with Dr. Carmichael and realized that MEDPREP was designed for students like Joe, Max, and me. It catered to students who had the knowledge and desire to go into medicine but who were underprepared for medical school. The three of us discussed the program, and we agreed that we would attend MEDPREP and overcome the MCAT hurdle together. That was the plan! We all applied, but only Max and I were accepted. This was definitely difficult for the three of us to deal with, but we continued to remain unified in our commitment to push one another until we all reached our goal of becoming physicians.

CHAPTER 6

Refuse to Fail

MEDPREP WAS A PROGRAM THAT God put in my path by design. The program was a yearlong grind of nonstop studying and working on our test-taking skills. Max and I would wake up in the early mornings and go to class, then spend our afternoons and evenings studying—often we were up until 1:00 a.m. or later.

MEDPREP offered automatic admission into SIU's College of Medicine for any student who passed the MCAT with a score of seven or higher in verbal reasoning, which is the section of the exam that tests reading comprehension. I knew this was my weakest area, so I read magazine articles daily and practiced passage after passage in an effort to improve my proficiency. Unfortunately, my verbal reasoning skills improved only marginally, although MEDPREP did improve my science proficiency. Nonetheless, my overall confidence improved immensely, and I retook the MCAT in April of 2003.

A few weeks later, I was at my mom's house when I got an email message saying my score was ready. My stomach dropped. I went to my room and closed the door. I had been disappointed so many times before that I did not want anyone around me when I saw my scores. Dropping down at my desk, I logged in, my eyes quickly scanning the page to find my score. My heart dropped into my stomach, and for a second, I felt as if something had stolen my breath. I stared at the results, seconds passing, as my mind raced with disbelief.

I had worked so hard. And still, I failed.

My poor performance on my second MCAT attempt was an unbelievably crushing blow. By this time, I had learned not to allow tests to define me as a person, but this was different: it seemed as if my world collapsed. Failing the exam after sacrificing an entire year of my life to this one singular goal put me into a deep depression. As overwhelmed and lost as I had felt during my first weeks at Xavier, I now felt ten times worse. I felt all the more alone and distraught because Max had performed very well on the exam, and Joe had created an alternate path for himself after not getting into MEDPREP. I was happy for them, of course, but lonely. I saw no realistic path to passing the MCAT, and I had no fallback plan for my future. For the first time, I started to allow defeat to consume me, even to the point of tears. I felt like a failure, and I began thinking that every person who had doubted my success had been right.

The reality of my failure was palpable. I questioned God, "Did you really bring me this far to fail?" I questioned myself, "Am I really smart enough to do this?" I was stuck in limbo. It's not in my nature to wallow in self-pity, but it took me a full week of praying and soul-searching to clear my mind and fight through my grief. I honestly didn't know what I could do at this point to improve my score.

My depression morphed quickly into anger. My MCAT score felt like an insult: it was telling me that I wasn't smart enough for medical school. I had been through too much in my life to let this exam defeat me, and I'd be damned if I let this one test cripple my destiny. I felt as though it was me against the world. The Omega quote, "The difficult I do immediately; the impossible takes but a second longer" became my rallying cry.

My girlfriend Michelle, who I had been dating for several months, was a major source of strength and guidance for me. We were an odd match—outside of medicine, our lives couldn't have been more different. Her father was a judge, her parents had been married for decades, and she had attended an affluent high school in the suburbs of Chicago before graduating from an elite California university. Michelle had done extremely well on the MCAT and had enrolled in MEDPREP to fulfill prerequisite courses for medical school that she hadn't taken as an undergraduate.

Despite Michelle's support, I couldn't help but be envious of her. I felt that I wouldn't have found myself in my current situation if I had even half the resources she was blessed with. Her dad was a role model who showed her how to succeed, whereas my dad was an addict who had abandoned me and who didn't even know that I was now going through the most difficult time of my life. This was a moment where my time in Omega Psi Phi carried me, for I drew strength from one of my pledge lessons, "Excuses are monuments of nothingness. They build bridges to nowhere. Those who use these tools of incompetence shall be masters of nothing."

I spent the summer studying with Michelle. She was one of the most well-organized people I had ever known. Every aspect of her life, from her daily schedule to her class notes, was always in perfect order. By contrast, my organizational skills had never evolved beyond my Trapper Keepers. It was during this summer that Michelle handed me the key to unlocking what was holding me back: basic disorganization. She taught me how to create a clear mind and a clear focus for each study session. For example, she introduced me to daily tasks and to-do lists that needed to be completed before hitting the books so that my mind was free from distractions. She showed me how to use file folders, color-coordinated labels, note cards, and electronic organizers to streamline my focus and stay on task.

Proper organization was invaluable to me. Now that I was organized, I began seeing redundancies and other flaws in my study tools. I realized the true importance of a clear and focused mind; the hundreds of little thoughts that had distracted me from my studies at any given moment were now all but eliminated. My scores on practice tests improved dramatically, even on the verbal section. By the end of the summer, I had morphed into a proficient test-taker.

When I took the MCAT for the third time in August of 2003, my confidence was at an all-time high. I remember the day clearly because I was so focused. My back was against the wall, yet I felt as confident as Michael Jordan in the fourth quarter. I breezed through the biological and physical science sections of the exam. Then came my archnemesis, the verbal reasoning section. SIU's automatic-acceptance score of seven loomed in my mind.

When the proctor started the verbal proficiency section, I began racing through the test's passages as feverishly as possible. Everything was going well until the proctor had a long coughing episode of five minutes or more midway through the section. Everything in me wanted to ask her to leave the room so that I could concentrate, but I knew she couldn't: leaving the room would invalidate the test. I completed the exam feeling a bit angry, but I was still confident that I had performed well.

When I received my grade, my overall performance alleviated any doubt about not being able to get into medical school. However, that medical school would probably not be SIU because I received only a six in verbal reasoning. Nonetheless, by doing well on the MCAT, I had overcome a hurdle that had been casting a shadow over the previous two years of my life. I was disappointed by not having achieved automatic acceptance into SIU, but I remembered my "no-excuses" lesson and trusted that God doesn't make mistakes.

With my MCAT score secure, I opted not to take the second year of study offered by MEDPREP and instead began directly applying to medical schools. I received a few declines, but many schools expressed interest in me and invited me to interview. I relished the process; interviewing created a huge sense of accomplishment in me. I scraped together the money to travel to interviews in New York; Iowa; Wisconsin; Washington, DC; Tennessee; and throughout Illinois. In total, I was accepted into six medical schools. I chose the University of Illinois College of Medicine, one of the largest medical schools in the country.

When applying to medical school, there's a gap year between acceptance and the time courses start. I chose to go back to Chicago to work and save money.

This was my first time living in Chicago in over five years. I quickly learned that a bachelor's degree in biology doesn't get you too many job offers. After a few weeks, I found myself still jobless and in need of money. I couldn't even earn money by cutting hair: since I had been away from Chicago for so long, all the people in the neighborhood who used my services were now going elsewhere for their haircuts. Fortunately, my friend Jerome introduced me to his father-in-law, Tom, who owned a barbershop. I did a demo haircut, and Tom offered me a position despite my not being a licensed barber.

Tom looked out for many good black men on the South Side who needed jobs. If you were skilled and hardworking, that's all Tom cared about. I feel that one of the major issues with the country today is that so many job opportunities are not offered to young black men. Most black men are looking for an honest living, yet there is an intrinsic societal racism that says all young black men are criminals: it's "expected" that we have records, even if we've never so much as received a speeding ticket. For those black men with teenage indiscretions or other small blemishes in their pasts, this can be disastrous—I've met several hardworking men with families who couldn't catch a break. A mistake doesn't make a man a criminal, yet this is one of the many biases black men face.

I had a bright and promising future, so many of the men working in the barbershop lived their dreams of success vicariously through me—society had killed their own dreams. However, I looked at these men as the true heroes: when society turned its back on them, they refused to give in to the temptation of illegal activity. They wanted better for themselves and better for their families. Being a barber is hard work, and it's a constant hustle for clients, but it's an honest living.

That year, I learned how to be a true barber, rather than merely a guy who knows how to cut hair. More importantly, I gained a better appreciation of the struggle of the black man in this world. I often had conversations about life with my fellow barbers. Listening to my friend Mike's story was compelling. He was in school at the University of Illinois with aspirations of becoming a physician. He was arrested for drug possession, which derailed his life and dreams. Here was a man who was an excellent father and a good man who made a mistake. Society was unforgiving and would not offer him a second chance. A young black man with a criminal record of any kind has minimal opportunity to show the world the good in him. I learned for the first time how blatantly society stereotypes and categorizes young black men. The owner of the barbershop would give jobs to out-of-work former felons, even though they did not have a barber's license, because he saw how badly they wanted to earn money legitimately and how society seemed to conspire to try to force them back behind bars. These men were not so different from me. They were fathers and brothers and husbands, good men who had made some bad choices. It was in that barbershop that I vowed never to change who I am and never to forget where I came from and to do my best to represent black men like them. Even today, I walk the halls of my hospital with my tattoos uncovered and diamond studs in my ears, specifically to challenge the stereotype of what a young black professional is "supposed" to look like: I am a young black doctor; the way I look doesn't make me a thug. When others encounter a young black man with a similar appearance, I want them to treat him with the same respect they would give to their doctor. Like I always say, I dream big.

A new barber in a new location always needs time to build clientele. In the meantime, I had bills to pay. I applied for a substitute teaching position with the CPS system. One of my first assignments was at Bond Elementary School in the South Side's Englewood neighborhood. On the first day, I was placed in a classroom full of students in grades six to eight, most of whom had learning disabilities or behavioral issues. None of the students could read above a fourth-grade level, and the eldest student, a sixteen-year-old, could barely read at all. The resources available were atrocious: students had to share books as I taught, and there were no structured lesson plans for me to model learning activities from. I was essentially thrown into this classroom and expected to figure it out.

I assumed that I could get through the day, then move on to the next assignment. But, to my initial dismay, my next assignment the following day was in the same classroom. By the third day, the kids had grown to like me and had started to look at me as a role model. At the end of that day, I was invited to teach the class for the remainder of the year. The thought of taking over this classroom without formal training was daunting. But I knew the system had turned its back on these students, and I wasn't going to do the same: if these kids couldn't have a highly trained education specialist to teach them, then at least they'd have a teacher who cared. For the rest of the year, I did the best job that I could do with the limited resources I had. By the end of the term, the kids loved me, and I loved them back.

This experience illustrates the inequality of Chicago's schools—and on a larger scale, of the country—that was apparent then and still present today: What are the career expectations for a sixteen-year-old black male who can't read? Does he have a fair shot at a professional career? Why are funds being poured into jails to prepare for his future, instead of using those funds to hire skilled teachers to help him learn?

Without a degree in teaching, there's no way I would have been hired as a teacher in a predominately white, affluent school in northern Chicago, yet on the South Side, I was hired to teach kids with special needs. As I worked with my students, I often asked myself, "If the odds are stacked against my becoming a doctor, how do I motivate these kids to overcome even larger hurdles?"

Teaching that year taught me that it's not enough for me just to be a role model: it's my duty to bring disparities in education to the forefront. Kids with limited educational resources must consistently compete against students from more affluent areas who are afforded a higher quality of education. To label underprivileged kids as failures in the face of prevalent educational disparities is insensitive and preposterous. I fully believe the key to creating more success stories for underprivileged students is to address disparities in the public school system, starting from grade school. All kids deserve the right to succeed in life; if more funding and resources go into the school systems of underserved communities, then stories like mine will be the norm and not the exception.

CHAPTER 7

From Historically Black to the Only Black

After I had decided on the University of Illinois as my school of choice, I then had to pick which track/campus I would enroll in. I had my choice of doing all four years of schooling in Chicago or doing my first year in Urbana–Champaign, then moving forward to either the Peoria campus or the Rockford campus.

Although I wanted desperately to attend the Chicago campus to be at home, I knew in my heart that living in Chicago would be setting myself up for failure because there would be too many distractions. One of the reasons I was successful at Xavier was because I had been freed from the daily responsibilities of helping my mom and being a father figure. This wouldn't be the case in Chicago, and deep down, I knew the challenge of caring for my family on top of medical school's rigorous curriculum would be too much to handle. Therefore, I chose to begin my education at the Urbana–Champaign campus, which was about two hours away from home.

I chose to commit to the Peoria tract for the last three years of my schooling mostly because of financial concerns. By choosing Peoria over Rockford, I could apply for free housing and would save over twenty thousand dollars. Financially, choosing the Peoria campus benefitted me the most, but I have doubts about whether it was the best decision for my success: I gravely underestimated just how difficult being the only African American male on Peoria's campus would be. The Rockford campus was more diverse, and maybe I wouldn't have faced so many biases there.

Medical school was the big stage, and the pressure was on. I was now at an institution where some of the most intelligent people in the world are tested. I can't lie and say that I didn't have doubts: Am I good enough to be here? Will I make it? Yet the competitor in me was ready for the challenge.

Now that I knew how to better organize myself and make the best possible use of my time, I knew my success would depend on using those tools and dedicating every possible minute to learning. I was in pure grind mode. In my experience, the University of Illinois College of Medicine was an old-school, hard-core academic environment that had no mercy on students who couldn't keep up—sadly, a student there had recently committed suicide because the pressure was too great.

My days were long, with lectures beginning at 8:00 a.m. and often running until after 4:00 p.m. This was not a good match for me because my attention span doesn't accommodate extensive focus over such long periods of time. However, I attended classes every day, no matter how long, then studied in the evenings.

But unlike most other students, I had additional pressure outside of just school. Living in Chicago meant that my family was once again at the forefront of my life—when my siblings wouldn't listen to my mother, she turned to me to be the disciplinarian. The most problematic kid was my younger brother Kyle. He was on the verge of being forced to repeat fourth grade because of his poor grades and behavior. My mother was deeply frustrated and was fearful of losing him to drugs, gangs, and violence.

My mother and I agreed that I would take guardianship of Kyle, and when I moved to Champaign, I brought him with me. Of course, I had some reservations—medical school was going to be uncharted waters, after all—but I hoped that a new environment and a strong male presence would force Kyle to turn his life around. So, Kyle and I moved into a small two-bedroom house I rented from my fraternity brother Reggie. Kyle had his own room, household chores, and all his responsibilities laid out for him. Homework was to be done as soon as he got home, and I adopted a no-nonsense policy about his behavior in school. When, two weeks into the school year, I learned that Kyle wasn't completing his homework, I held him accountable and provided him structure in a way my mother had not been able to. He was an A and B student for the rest of the year, and he even made the honor roll.

Kyle's drastically improved grades and behavior exemplify the importance of a father figure in a child's life. The influence of strong African American males in the lives of so many of our children is lacking, which is why children are so often misguided. Individuals outside of my race often point out that I "made it" despite the lack of a father; I'm often asked, "Why can't others do what you did?" It's a difficult question to answer. All I can say is that there aren't too many fatherless kids who are afforded the blessings that I was given. So, to compare me to other black kids without father figures who grew up in poverty and struggle because of it is simply unfair. I am an exception—but not because I was better than other kids. Most children like me simply cannot overcome all of these obstacles, and they should not have to.

While I was glad to do this for my brother, it took time that I should have been using to study. So, in order to balance my responsibilities as a guardian with my studies, I strictly adhered to a parenting schedule that I created for Kyle.

Even though medical school presented me with a huge amount of material to digest, I was learning a lot and generally feeling comfortable with my retention skills and my mastery of the material. However, as I sat through the first few tests, one major problem became evident: time. There were numerous occasions when I had barely passed an exam's halfway point, only to hear the proctor call out, "Ten minutes remaining." At that point, panic would set in, and the rest of the exam became a blur. The more I tried to speed up my thinking, the poorer my performance. I went to student affairs for help, but because this wasn't a common problem among students in the program, I found little sympathy or assistance.

Medical school was completely different from my undergraduate experience. When asked for help at Xavier, no stone was left unturned, and I received the assistance I needed. The University of Illinois didn't offer nearly the same support. At first, the people in student affairs told me that I simply needed to study more, but I knew that wasn't the underlying problem, so I continued to pressure the administration for help. Midway through my first year, I was finally sent for an evaluation: it was determined that I had attention deficit hyperactivity disorder (ADHD), and it was recommended that I get extra time on exams. Once I was given extra time, my testing issues disappeared.

To this day, I still contend that answering test questions quickly has nothing to do with a physician's true ability. Yes, doctors must be able to make split-second decisions effectively and accurately when needed, but the real-world application of these skills is very different from parsing test questions. For instance, during my first year in private practice, I was called to the emergency room to assess a woman with a gunshot wound to the neck; she was thirty-eight weeks pregnant. The vascular surgeons on staff were trying desperately to stabilize her, but she was losing blood quickly. As the ob-gyn on call, I had to pinpoint the exact moment to deliver the baby via cesarean. If I acted while the patient was still hemorrhaging, I would've probably saved the baby but lost the mother. Conversely, if I waited too long to intervene, I would have risked losing the baby secondary to placental insufficiency from lack of blood flow. As soon as the bleeding was reasonably under control, I performed the cesarean and closed in less than eleven minutes, leaving the vascular team free to finish their work. (Both mother and baby are doing excellent today.) No exam in creation could have prepared me for that day or could have predicted my ability to make split-second clinical decisions while remaining calm under pressure.

I successfully passed my first year in medical school, and Kyle finished the school year on the honor roll. For the remainder of medical school, I moved to the Peoria campus, and Kyle moved back to Chicago with my mother. My main reason for choosing Peoria was the free housing, but what I didn't realize at the time was how stressful being the only African American student in my class would be. At Xavier, one of the nation's historically black colleges and universities (HBCUs), I had been surrounded by students with whom I had things in common and who had experienced struggles similar to mine; in Peoria, I was a man on an island. I didn't even have Michelle by my side anymore; she'd been accepted to a medical school in Texas, and we were growing apart.

The only person I formed a bond with in Peoria was Pete, a white student from a suburb just north of Chicago. He was a bit of a social butterfly and got along well with everybody. He accepted that we were from two totally different backgrounds and, more importantly, respected our differences. Of course, some of my other classmates were respectful, too, but Pete actively took an interest in learning more about me and my culture, and he did so without arrogance or entitlement.

One of the tenets of medical school is that students should study in groups and form support systems. Pete was a good friend, but unfortunately, we couldn't study together: he was an abstract thinker, whereas I was an analytical one. We tried to study together a few times, but it quickly became evident that we weren't a good match. We couldn't even share notes because Pete had the ability to absorb information without having to write too much down. Additionally, he preferred to study alone, and I respected that. However, since I had always thrived from studying in groups, this hurt a bit. I didn't have anyone else to turn to for support: the color of my skin and the culture from which I came meant that I was never truly accepted by my peers.

Institutionalized racism was alive and well on campus. Most of my classmates showed little to no interest in getting to know me. The overall assumption, particularly from white students, was that learning about black culture was a waste of time—most of my classmates felt no obligation to black culture and had even less interest in learning about it.

When Hurricane Katrina hit New Orleans in 2005, and the mistreatment of African Americans was put on display for the world to see, I began to focus even more on the biased behaviors and attitudes of my classmates. It was one thing for them not to share their notes or welcome me into their study groups, but racist and ignorant remarks were another thing altogether. I heard many future doctors make repeated, insensitive comments about minorities that enraged me to my core. Later on, when Barack Obama was running for president in 2008, I saw one of my classmates wearing an "Obama is my homeboy" T-shirt. This sent me over the edge—such condescension toward the first African American presidential nominee was the final straw that broke the camel's back. After confronting this student's disrespect, I went to the administration and pushed for cultural competency training for all students. I could do little, personally, to challenge the hearts and minds of other students, but through education, the administration had the opportunity to create a real and lasting impact.

During this second year of school, the academic rigors became even more demanding. I was up late studying every night, which left me dead tired during the day. I didn't dare skip classes to rest because there weren't any students who would lend me their notes. One day, with my books spread out all around me, I fell asleep in a nephrology lecture. The professor, Dr. Horvath, had told us on the first day of class that studying his notes would be all we needed to do to pass the course. However, because renal was one of the hardest subjects for me, I was using every textbook I could find in an attempt to grasp the material.

After the lecture, Dr. Horvath tapped me on my shoulder to wake me up. He was stunned by all the open textbooks on my desk and asked, "Didn't I tell you that my notes are all you need for this class?" As I quickly tried to pull myself together, I groggily told him that I didn't understand the material and was supplementing because "I need all the help I can get." From there, Dr. Horvath took me to lunch, and we had a long conversation. He was amazed at my background and my path to medical school, and I was astounded that he took time out of his schedule to talk with me.

From that day forth, Dr. Horvath took me under his wing and served as my mentor. We formed a lifelong friendship. Like George Goewey, Dr. Horvath proved to me that compassion and love have no color. He made no judgments on the basis of my skin: all he saw was a distraught student who needed some extra guidance and support. I am forever grateful to him.

I never quite got used to being alone in medical school, and in my second year, I started visiting Chicago whenever I could. The drive was long, but if I managed my time carefully during the week, I could sometimes go home on the weekends. I'd known Danielle my entire life—in fact, her mother was my brother Elliot's godmother—but we'd never had an interest in each other romantically. One Sunday after church, all that changed.

We moved extremely fast. Within a month, Danielle had moved to Peoria with me. At first, she provided the support and companionship that I needed. I knew I wasn't ready to live with someone, but she made me happy. We weren't as careful with our birth control as we should have been, and within a few months, we were looking at a positive pregnancy test.

My mind raced with mixed emotions. I had a hundred questions: Could I be the father I knew I needed to be while pursuing my medical degree? How would a child and a family affect my future? Could we manage to live comfortably enough on my student loans until I started my paid residency? Emotionally, I knew I wasn't ready to marry and raise a family. My romantic relationship with Danielle was still very new, and in a way, we were starting over—our lives had totally diverged during my college years. But at this point, I was now twenty-six years old, and abortion was no longer an option: I was going to give fatherhood 110 percent. I vowed that my relationship with my child would be nothing like my relationship with my own father. I would be a strong father and would set a good example.

The first ultrasound changed my life forever. Danielle and I were with the sonographer when she looked at us and asked, "Are y'all trying to keep me in here all day?" We were confused by the question until the sonographer flipped the monitor toward us and we clearly saw two little fetuses with two fluttering heartbeats. I nearly fell out of my seat! I now had to figure out how to handle life's curve ball quickly, and all the calculations I'd made for one child had to be thrown out the window. It took me a few weeks to process all this, but once reality set in, I appreciated the blessing of being a father.

The impending arrival of twins would have been complicated enough for any man, but at this point, I was also studying feverishly for the United States Medical Licensing Examination (USMLE) Step 1. The first USMLE exam is by far the hardest of the three; most often, when second-year medical students drop out of school, it's due to an inability to pass this first test. At most medical schools, students are not allowed to continue with their studies until they have passed the USMLE Step 1, and the University of Illinois was no different.

That summer, when Danielle moved in, I was studying as hard as I could—sometimes as much as twenty hours a day with minimal breaks—because I didn't want to relive my MCAT nightmare. Danielle was a big help; without her, I might've gone days without eating a proper meal. She was my sole support system during this time of solitude. The USMLE Step 1 would be the test of my life; extra time for slow test takers was not allowed, so I had the additional challenge of trying to figure out ways of improving my completion times for each section.

I went into the exam focused, prepared, organized, and determined not to be a victim of the dreaded Step 1. I was relieved after I completed the test, but I knew it would be up to six weeks before receiving my score. The stress of waiting was almost unbearable—fear of failure woke me up at night. I felt proud of my accomplishments up to that point, but I also knew that failing Step 1 had the potential to alter my entire life and derail my career. I was also still processing the reality of being a father to two children and trying to prepare myself for the major adjustments I would have to make as a father. Every day, I woke up in a panic, like a kid going outside at recess to face a bully.

My USMLE score was still pending when I started my third year of medical school, which is when students begin rotations in areas such as family medicine, pediatrics, obstetrics, and others. My long days of sitting at a desk and listening to lectures were now behind me. Rotations were the moment when I felt I would finally shine: I would never have the best test scores in the class, but I knew I had the life experiences that would help me to relate to patients.

I put my best foot forward daily—not only because I wanted to learn all that I could but also because, as the only black medical student, I knew that I had a bull's-eye on my back. I understood that every move I made would be scrutinized and that I would have to outperform my counterparts on a daily basis just to have a chance of receiving a fair grade. I showed up early, stayed late, and read case files feverishly so that I was prepared for any and every question asked of me. When an attending doctor asked us questions, I always tried to be the first to answer. When I spoke, I made sure I was always professional and kept my slang terms to a minimum. Without brownnosing, I treated every attending and all the senior residents with the utmost respect. I wanted my superiors to know that I was respectful but confident.

I was midway through my family medicine rotation when I received a page. I knew the news had to be bad because the page was from the school's administrative office and not the hospital itself. I took several long, deep breaths before phoning the office, but in my gut, I already knew what the issue was: I had failed the USMLE Step 1. My heart sank, and my mind started racing. I gave everything that I had to that test—there were no more available hours to study in a day. Plus, the birth of my children was coming that much closer. How in the world was I going to focus on retaking the test with all of the added stress?

I immediately went to the administration to discuss my results—and my future. I had failed the exam by only one point; passing was 183, and I had scored a 182. Was my life really ruined over one question? Frustration and disbelief took over. I even became angry for a short period and sincerely wondered if there was a conspiracy against me. As I look back now, I laugh at my conspiracy-theory thoughts, but they felt real and true in the moment. I was suspended from my clinical rotations immediately, per the university's policy.

I went back to my apartment deflated and depressed. I didn't know where to turn at that point and felt more isolated than ever. Danielle tried to offer some words of comfort, but I didn't want to talk. I cried myself to sleep, hoping all the while that I could sleep off this nightmare. I thought to myself, "How will my classmates judge me?" In my head, everyone who had ever believed that I wasn't smart enough to get through this process was saying, "I told you!"

God is always doing amazing works, but it isn't until we find ourselves in difficult times that we truly realize His grace. The day after I received the news of my failure, Joe called me: he had failed the USMLE Step 1 by two points. On the one hand, I was upset for him because he was my brother, and I wanted him to succeed; however, I was also rejuvenated because I now had a friend who could relate to how I was feeling. I was no longer alone. We talked for several hours that day.

By the end of our conversation, Joe and I found a new motivation in each other. We agreed that Joe would come to Peoria for a month of intensive study. Max had passed the exam, and we were very happy for him, but we couldn't bask in the glory with him. Instead, Joe and I had a mission to complete together. We would draw strength and confidence from each other and devote ourselves to test prep. If we leaned on each other, I knew we could both achieve a passing grade.

Like me, Joe also had a family to consider; he had a young son and was engaged to his future wife. We never neglected responsibilities, but our families had to accept that studying would be our absolute priority for at least a month.

I arranged short-term housing for Joe with my fraternity brother Brian; my apartment was already too cramped. Every day, I picked Joe up at 7:00 a.m., and we would study together and drill each other. When I dropped him off each night, we prayed together. We asked God to have mercy on us and to let us gain the knowledge and understanding needed to achieve our goals. Joe and I already considered each other brothers, but during this month, our bond strengthened tenfold.

God works in ways that are often difficult to appreciate when we are in the midst of tribulation. At the time, Joe and I couldn't understand why God allowed both of us to fail by such a small margin. I now understand that God gave us those scores to tell us that we could both pass—but only if we did so together. Had one of us passed the test the first time, it may have forever changed the course of the individual who failed. Our failure on Step 1 positively impacted both our lives: without that initial failure, our bond never would have been refortified. I am thankful and wouldn't have it any other way. The experience is the perfect example of how failures don't define our lives: we are defined by our responses to those failures.

After a month of rigorous studying, Joe returned home to his family. We both took the exam shortly thereafter and passed with flying colors. With my passing USMLE score, I was able to resume my clinical rotations. I returned to my rotations with the same energy and enthusiasm that I had before retaking Step 1, but I also spoke with the physicians who led each of my clinical teams and arranged my schedule so that I could attend every prenatal appointment with Danielle, especially since the sex of our children would soon be known. I wanted twin boys because I feared the future of raising two teenage girls; the thought of protecting them from the dangers of the world seemed overwhelming. When the ultrasound showed fraternal twins, a boy and a girl, I breathed a sigh of relief—at least my daughter would have a brother to help protect her when she wasn't with me.

It wasn't until the following ultrasound a few weeks later that our doctor spotted an abnormality with my son's heart and sent us to see a specialist in maternal-fetal medicine. The specialist diagnosed my baby boy with a congenital heart defect, Tetralogy of Fallot. As a medical student, I knew Tetralogy of Fallot meant that my son's heart couldn't provide enough oxygenated blood to his body, but as a father, I was frightened and clueless because I couldn't envision the impact this would have on my child. The physicians who cared for Danielle and our growing babies explained everything in detail and were extremely supportive. They couldn't alleviate all of our concerns, of course, but we were comfortable in knowing that everything possible would be done for our son.

The personal life of a medical student cannot affect his clinical duties. Despite the issues I was having at home, I remained respectful to my superiors, presented myself very professionally, and gave my all to learning and taking care of patients. But the one thing I refused to do was change myself: I never softened my exterior or adopted a subservient persona to make my superiors feel more comfortable with me. I wore a single diamond earring in each ear daily. I believe in "dressing for success," so I always had a dress shirt with a tie under my white lab coat, whereas many of my peers wore polo shirts or other business-casual attire. I was in good shape too—I was in the gym regularly that year—and that boosted my confidence. What I learned is that there are many people, especially white men, who are intimidated by a strong, confident black man. Although I was respectful and professional, my reviews usually included some form of negative comment about my appearance that marginalized me.

My ob-gyn rotation was especially difficult due to these prejudices. One of the third-year residents on my team, a young white male, was very condescending toward me and took every opportunity to try to prove his superiority. At the same time, our attending was consistently short with me, and although she never said anything to me directly, she complained to her peers about my appearance. For example, I was told that she complained about me because "in her culture, only women wear earrings." I had to double my focus in order to ignore all of this negativity. Nonetheless, I did learn a lot in my ob-gyn rotation, and my desire to be an ob-gyn never wavered. Specifically, I learned a lot about the vast number of surgeries that gynecologists perform. I watched as physicians used scalpels and scissors in complex surgeries, and this is when I realized that my precision skills with my hands would be very useful in surgery. I became even more intrigued with the specialty. To me, it seemed the perfect mix of clinical service, surgery, and obstetric care.

One of the most blatantly racist events in my medical school experience—and indeed, in my entire life—occurred during my surgical rotation. By the time I started this rotation, I had already completed three or four other rotations, including my ob-gyn service. I was particularly excited about the surgical rotation because I didn't have the opportunity to operate much during my time with the ob-gyn staff, and I wanted to enhance my surgical skills.

My first two weeks on the surgical team were in the trauma service. Surgery was set up differently from other rotations; senior residents ran the trauma service, and therefore third-year students had little interaction with "attending physicians". The chief resident on the trauma service was a fifty-three-year-old white man who was a former pastor. Late in life, he had received a revelation that had called him to medicine. Before I even met this man, I felt optimistic when I heard that he was a former pastor—and I always admire those who are brave enough to switch careers in pursuit of their dreams. I figured that if anyone would give me a fair chance, it would be him.

My surgical team had only three members: the chief resident, Dr. R.; a first-year surgical resident, Dr. P.; and myself. From the first day, I could sense that something was very wrong. The chief resident would speak to Dr. P. directly while acting as if I were invisible. When I asked a question, only Dr. P. would answer me, and the few times that Dr. R. did speak to me, he refused to look me in the eye. I vividly remember one morning after rounds when the chief resident purposely excluded me while he was reviewing patient cases with Dr. P. At first, I shook the mistreatment off and chose to focus on doing the best job that I could do. As long as I didn't blow up and remained respectful, I thought

I could get through the two weeks and move on. I truly did my best to do just that, until one afternoon in the operating room.

After any surgery, medical students were expected to help the ancillary staff move the patient from the operating table to the transport bed. This was an unwritten rule of the operating room, and I had no problem doing this because it helped the patient—and in any case, it was part of the process of paying my dues. Yet one afternoon, as we were about to lift the patient onto the transport bed, the chief resident said to me, "Pierre, this is where a strong body and a small mind are put to good use."

It took everything I had inside of me to remain calm and keep myself from exploding in sheer rage. The tone of his voice reminded me of the scene in *Roots* when the overseer whipped Kunta Kinte into acknowledging his slave name of Toby. This from a man who had never even asked me a question to gauge my knowledge, who could barely deign to speak to me! I turned around and stared at him. I was so infuriated that I knew anything I said would be inflammatory and extremely inappropriate for a professional environment. I knew how quickly this could escalate: I could picture the chief resident saying something even more racist in response, and at that point, it would've become entirely possible for me to lose all decorum and put my hands on him. Yet, as a strong black man, I knew this bigot wasn't worth my getting kicked out of school and ruining my life. He would always see me as only good for moving patients; in his eyes, I would never be a "real" doctor.

This is a major teaching moment that I want to give black kids. Think out every situation, and understand the consequences and ramifications of every action. Dreams can be derailed in a split second with an impulsive decision. Keeping my cool in this moment probably saved my entire career. It's an unfortunate truth that black men in this country are not "allowed" to question authority or stand up for our rights; doing so while enraged only makes voicing our very valid concerns seem all the more threatening to those in positions of authority or power. As black men, this is yet another challenge we face; allowing ourselves to act on impulse will almost always have inequitably harsh and potentially devastating consequences. This is true in every facet of our lives, not just on the job—you need only ask the families of Amadou Diallo, Manuel

Loggins Jr., Ramarley Graham, Eric Garner, Tamir Rice, Laquan McDonald, Michael Brown Jr., Samuel DuBose, and Philando Castile.[7]

Later that same day, I met with the program director about my concerns. I explained to him that the chief resident had a problem with me and said I wanted to be removed from the service. I stopped short of calling this man a bigot: I knew that talking about race makes people uncomfortable, and all I wanted to do was get through the rotation and be graded fairly. The program director told me not to worry about it, then added that students were paired with multiple physicians so that we could receive many different evaluations. Because I had presented my concerns, I felt that I had adequately covered myself against any racist evaluations. I was wrong.

I suffered through the rest of the two weeks on the trauma team, then moved to the next service, which was run by different residents. Except for those first two weeks, my surgical rotation was a great experience. I scored extraordinarily well on my exit exam and even had hopes of passing the surgical rotation with my first high grade.

I was in total shock when I saw my surgical rotation grade: incomplete. I immediately set up a meeting with the surgical department's chairman and the clerkship director. They presented me with my file. The very first review was chief resident's, which was a full three pages long. He had ripped my performance to shreds. Dr. R., who had never even had a real conversation with me, criticized even the smallest events that he had "witnessed," then went into elaborate detail about how he felt about me as a student. One could argue that his review was an honest assessment of my performance—if it weren't for the very last sentence. To quote from his review, "I was concerned about sharing my opinions about Pierre due to any cultural biases that I may have against him, but I discussed my concerns with several of the attending physicians, and they reassured me that my concerns are valid."

---

7 Among many other sources, supporting information can be found at the websites of the *Los Angeles Times* and the *New York Times*, respectively; see http://www.latimes.com/nation/la-na-police-deaths-20160707-snap-htmlstory.html#2016 and http://www.nytimes.com/video/us/100000004517374/deadly-police-shooting-in-minnesota.html.

When I read that line, I was infuriated. I couldn't believe that the hospital's administrators would accept the opinion of an admitted racist and punish me, and I immediately went to the school's administration. After a series of meetings, the chairman of the surgical program got angry. He tried to scold me as if I were a child: he told me I needed to accept my punishment and be quiet. He proposed I perform a remediation plan that would be created by him, and he informed me that if I continued to argue, he would fail me outright and require me to repeat the entire rotation. Because I had already taken extra time to retake the USMLE Step 1, I was already precariously close to not graduating on time; I had no choice but to accept remediation.

This situation is the perfect example of how white men in power in America can be intimidated by young black men. In my case, I wasn't brutalized physically, but I was pushed into submissiveness and "obedience." I was given a grade that I didn't deserve and forced to spend a month shadowing a general surgeon in a rural town. Worse still, the surgeon I was to assigned to shadow was in Pontiac, over an hour away from Peoria.

Remediation meant that I had to leave Danielle behind in her third trimester. I was incredibly unhappy living alone in Pontiac, but I met a few good people along the way, including Dr. Proehl. Dr. Proehl was a kind man who held no prejudices against the color of my skin. He worked with me one-on-one and taught me many valuable lessons, all of which helped to improve my surgical skills. I am thankful for my time with him.

My anticipation of the birth of my children grew to epic proportions in the weeks leading to their delivery. Our high-risk pregnancy specialist, Dr. Renfroe, decided the twins should be delivered via cesarean to avoid putting stress on my son's heart. Pierre M. Johnson II and Piersyn L. Johnson were born on Valentine's Day, 2007. Piersyn was born healthy, and I thanked God for that blessing, but my primary focus was on Pierre and his heart. Although all signs at birth were positive, he was immediately placed in intensive care so that he could be closely monitored. I don't think that I slept for the entire first two days. I stayed up and watched my baby boy, terrified of even the smallest sign of distress. Fortunately, my son never turned blue or showed any other signs of distress. Danielle and the twins were discharged after five days in the hospital. At that moment, nothing mattered more than that—my babies were OK.

CHAPTER 8

Everything Is Earned

Even with all the stress going on at home, my third year as a medical student came to a successful close. I had completed all my rotations and passed the corresponding tests. The start of my fourth year flew by, and I passed the USMLE Step 2 without issue. All I needed now was to be accepted into a residency program to fulfill my ultimate dream of becoming an ob-gyn.

Through the match system, I was invited to interview with nine different programs. I attended every interview. Of course, I had my favorite programs, but truly, all I wanted was to be accepted into an ob-gyn residency. Given my high number of interviews, I was fairly confident that I would match somewhere. But when the match results came in, I discovered, to my dismay, that I didn't match anywhere.

This is the worst news I could have received! Not only did I need a match to complete my education, but with two new babies, I also needed the salary that came with a residency. At the time, I had no idea what had gone wrong. Much later, I learned that my USMLE Step 2 score was never sent with my residency applications; the score was listed as pending in my file. This, in conjunction with my having initially failed Step 1, made residency programs apprehensive about my abilities. I received many invitations to interview because of the promise I showed, but ultimately, my rankings were not high. I won't say my pending Step 2 score was the sole reason why I didn't match into an ob-gyn residency, but I'm sure it played a significant role.

Without a residency match, I was placed in "the scramble." The scramble was a free-for-all in which students without residency homes actively searched for positions. We were given the listings for all program openings in every specialty because unmatched students often had to choose undesired specialties. Residents are allowed to transfer to another specialty later on, but it is extremely difficult to do so.

The scramble room was set up like a call center; students were given a telephone and a desk. The first day, I called every ob-gyn program listed, but I was unsuccessful. As I watched the few available ob-gyn residencies quickly fill up, I knew I had to think of a viable alternative. I decided the best course was to try for a general surgery residency, then reapply next year for an ob-gyn position.

I used every resource I could. I asked Dr. Renfroe and Dr. Horvath to make calls on my behalf. I even gave a scramble list to Danielle so that she could place calls for me from home. By the end of the second day, I was utterly dejected. I felt embarrassed because most of my classmates had matched and were celebrating their new positions. By the third day, I asked God, "Is this part of your plan?" as a hundred other questions swarmed in my mind: How would I support my family? Should I find a research position for a year, then reapply for residency the year after? What if the same thing happened next year? I was at the lowest point of my life; I was terrified and depressed. I felt like I had traveled down a hundred-mile road just to find a dead end. At this point, I was willing to accept a residency in any field. I prayed and hoped that I would get through what felt like my darkest hour.

All of a sudden, Danielle called me in pure excitement. She told me to call Mrs. Montgomery, the program coordinator for general surgery at the Washington Hospital Center in DC. Mrs. Montgomery interviewed me briefly, then put me in touch with Dr. Boyle, the general surgery program director. As I spoke to Dr. Boyle, all I was hoping for was a chance to prove myself. After a few minutes of discussion, Dr. Boyle accepted me as a resident.

Just like that, at my lowest moment, God made a way from no way. I had never even heard of the Washington Hospital Center, nor would I ever have imagined that I'd be doing my residency in a general surgery program there. In retrospect, I wouldn't have changed anything about my residency-match process, except perhaps for the three days of anguished waiting. But even that had a purpose: God wanted to show me that He has total control of my life and my future. If I hadn't hit rock bottom, I would never have been fully able to appreciate success.

Everything about the move to Washington, DC, felt right except two major reasons against it: Pierre and Piersyn. Fatherhood was now my most important obligation, especially now that Danielle and I had broken off our engagement. The twins were only a year old, and I felt like leaving them at this age would make me a neglectful father. On the other hand, if I declined the residency, what would my future look like? More importantly, how would I provide for my children? Moving eight hundred miles away from my babies was one of the toughest decisions of my life, but in the end, I knew it was the right choice. I would have to accept being away for a year so that I could provide a better life for my children in the future.

My surgical experience at Washington Hospital Center transformed my career. I worked firsthand with highly skilled general surgeons and surgery residents. I had the opportunity to work one-on-one with skilled reconstructive surgeons for a full quarter of that year. The staff there was highly diverse; I no longer felt like a man on an island but rather—for the first time since entering medical school—as a part of the team. Washington Hospital Center was a large hospital, and my caseload was demanding, but I effectively managed all my responsibilities as a resident. I hated being away from the twins, but I reminded myself that this was temporary: I would be back in Illinois soon with a full year's experience on my résumé, and I would then, with any luck, be able to match into a local ob-gyn residency.

I worked hard that entire year to learn as much as I possibly could. In addition to learning the best practices for general surgery, I also learned how to care for patients who required complex surgeries, as well as for those patients who had complications. I also met a phenomenal woman, Erin, who would support me through the next phase of my residency path. Erin was a nurse at the hospital where I worked. She was smart and ambitious and supported me as I struggled against discrimination and self-doubt. I thank God for not matching me into an ob-gyn residency the first time around because I would not have met Erin, and I wouldn't be half the surgeon I am today if not for my experience at Washington Hospital Center.

When I reapplied for ob-gyn residencies at the end of the year, I had an entirely new type of confidence; I knew I'd now be seen as an asset to any program, and I was invited to interview for ten different openings. I was particularly focused on an ob-gyn residency at SIU; after not being auto-accepted into SIU due to my MCAT score in verbal reasoning, I wanted to prove that I belonged in the SIU medical program.

I had interviewed with SIU on my first round of residency applications. At that time, I had an in-depth conversation with the chairman of the ob-gyn program, Dr. Loret de Mola; he had been intrigued by me being a barber. He'd never had a barber apply to the program, and he had challenged me to research the historical link between barbers and surgeons. When I met Dr. Loret de Mola during my second residency search in 2009, I was fully prepared with talking points on the origins of surgery and how my unique skill set would be an asset to the program.

I got my wish and matched with SIU, but my residency was tough—well beyond the challenge of any residency. As I looked at the wall showing all of the medical school graduates since the program started in the 1970s, I saw several black women on the graduate photo wall. If I graduated, I would be the very first black man to do so. Most people think about racism in terms of police brutality, white supremacy, or other overt examples. Certainly, such overt racism was all around me; my first year in Springfield was also the year that Barack Obama became president of the United States, and in response to America's first black president, hate crimes were on the rise in Illinois. Among other incidents, a noose was hung on the grounds of a Springfield utility, and the state building housing the Black Caucus was vandalized with hate speech.[8]

I also had to face professional racism daily. Institutionalized racism in a professional setting can be difficult to prove, but it's insidious nonetheless. SIU's

8 Further information is available at the website of the *Illinois Times*, http://illinoistimes.com/article-7082-noose-incidents-spark-hate-symbols-bill.html.

hospital was small and very homogeneous racially. As an African American in a position of authority, anyone with even the slightest racial bias could take aim at me. In Washington, DC, I'd never had any complaints from the ancillary staff, yet during my residency in central Illinois, at a hospital one-third the size of the Washington Hospital Center, I was reprimanded by the administration countless times for allegedly not answering pages from the ancillary staff. I was constantly in conflict with nurses who second-guessed my judgment as a resident—a few of these nurses would outright refuse to follow through on any of my orders. Even my peers made it a point to marginalize me in subtle ways. All complaints about me were taken seriously and came with consequences, but my program director refused to acknowledge my concerns regarding bias.

I had no choice but to persevere through my four residency years at SIU; no one was going to get in the way of my goals, and no one was going to make me fundamentally change myself for the sake of his or her own comfort. Neither the color of my skin nor the earrings in my ears have anything to do with the capacity of my mind, my years of specialized training, or my ability to improve the lives of my patients. SIU was my last hurdle; I still loved my specialty, I was still passionate about providing medical care to women, and no one was going to rob me of that.

CHAPTER 9

Living My Dream

AFTER FOUR LONG RESIDENCY YEARS, I moved into private practice at an ob-gyn group in Decatur, Illinois. My immediate focus was to remain close to my children, who were in school in the area. Ultimately, however, my goal was to return to Chicago and make an impact on the community that I grew up in. Decatur offered me a lucrative opportunity and valuable experience that I could use as a base while putting my plans for returning to Chicago in motion.

Once again, in 2015, I found myself waiting for the results of a test that would determine my future. I had to pass my boards in order to become certified in obstetrics and gynecology. This time when the notice of the results landed in my inbox, I was in my office at the hospital. I braced myself for yet another disappointment. Then I saw the word I was looking for: passed. I was now certified by the American Board of Obstetrics and Gynecology. That's when it hit me; all of the years of sacrifice, all of the years of struggle, and my dreams finally came to fruition. In fact, I got a tattoo on my shoulder shortly after this of a man kneeling, holding up the globe. The weight of the world was lifted off my shoulders. Accomplishing any goal is always satisfying, but fulfilling your lifelong dream is the most liberating feeling that can be attained. I didn't need that score to validate all of my hard work and sacrifice, but I needed to give myself the inner peace that I had been striving for all of my life. A smile spread across my face, and I hurriedly called Joe, who had not taken his boards yet. I texted Max and my mom as relief and then exuberance washed over me. After all of the years of struggle, the failures and frustrations, I could finally breathe easily. I had made it over the final hurdle.

As a physician, I specialize in both minimally invasive gynecologic surgery and pelvic floor repair, as well as in high-risk obstetrics. I'm specially trained in high-tech gynecological procedures. After three years in private practice, I was presented with the opportunity to take over an established practice in the Chicagoland area, where I still work today. In 2016, as I was in the process of writing this book, I received the highest accreditation possible in my field: I am now a Fellow of the American Congress of Obstetricians and Gynecologists. My dreams as a young man are now a reality that I live every day. I survived the storm without compromising my sense of self or my culture. So remember: that young black guy with Jordans and tattoos may very well be the surgeon who saves your life.

Although I am proud of my accomplishments, complacency will never be a part of my mind-set. I know that I have much more work to do to if I'm to truly effect change in areas like the South Side. So often, African Americans have to put significant extra effort into achieving professional success, yet once these goals are achieved, they rest on their own laurels without giving back to the neighborhoods of their youth. This is a sad reality but also a large part of why our communities remain stagnant in mediocrity.

As I move forward, I want to positively impact underrepresented communities in two very important ways. The first is through medicine and community outreach. For many years, I have aspired to establish large community outreach clinics (COCs) throughout the country, starting in Chicago. I want to partner with physicians, social workers, educators, counselors, and financial planners to provide services aimed at strengthening families. Access to affordable, effective health care makes an enormous difference in the stability of any home, but I also seek to strengthen families themselves through my COCs. Through all my years of training, I learned that the majority of successful individuals come from well-structured families that support the pursuit of excellence. For many children of underprivileged communities, this family structure and support has all but disappeared, and so many of our children face overwhelming—and oftentimes insurmountable—obstacles with little guidance and minimal support, just as I did. My COCs will offer a refuge for young people who need advice and direction, medical treatment, counseling, or other services. We will not only care for that scared, pregnant teenage girl but will offer parental counseling focused on effective, engaged parenting to that young teenage boy who is about to become a father. In communities like mine, where mother-headed single-parent households are increasingly becoming the norm, too often, the importance of fathers is minimized to solely providing child support, when fatherhood should be about so much more than that. Worse, children who grow up without an engaged father figure are more likely to perpetuate the same cycle when they begin creating their own families.

The second way that I plan to impact the lives of others is through public speaking. Joe, Max, and I believe that this book is only the beginning. We want to share the trials and tribulations we have overcome with people all over the country. Each of us is a living testimony: all goals and dreams can be achieved with the right mind-set, no matter where you come from. All three of us were "expected" to fail because of our race and underprivileged backgrounds, yet all of us have achieved exactly what we set out to do as young men. Additionally, we are in strong agreement that fatherhood is our first and foremost responsibility, and we witness daily how our children benefit from the strong examples we set. We hope to provide similar influence and inspiration for others.

Each of us is a living example that even if you come from the worst of circumstances, you can still achieve your goals and dreams. But importantly, our stories also show that achieving these dreams will not be easy; you may fail more times than you succeed, and it will often feel as if the world is against you, especially if you are black.

Our testimony is simple: When you are black in America, the odds are not going to be in your favor. Succeed anyway.

BOOK II

Maxime's Story

Foreword

If my late grandparents were alive to witness the life I have built, they would definitely say that I am "blessed and highly favored." In many ways, they would be right; by most accounts, I now live a privileged life. Yet this life is reflective of decades of hard work and perseverance. Certainly, there have been obstacles in my life, and certainly, some seemed insurmountable. Yet as I look back, I realize there has always been a higher power playing a substantial role in getting me to this point. I thank God every single day for allowing me to have the clarity of thought at those critical junctures where my story could have unfolded very differently. Today, I write this book for my children. I hope my story will help them to know their father better while teaching them to recognize the higher power in their own lives.

As I write this, I feel the weight of what it means to tell my story honestly. Honesty inherently means vulnerability. What if sharing my life's path leaves me exposed to public ridicule and judgment? I am a bit of an introvert, after all, and sharing my personal experiences so publicly leaves me with a feeling of discomfort. I feel, on some level, like a child on his very first day at a new school—no one knows me, and all I want is to be accepted for who I am, even though the fear of rejection looms.

From the outside looking in, it may look as if I've achieved the American dream. Today I have a wonderful wife, three beautiful children, a nice house, and I'm a board-certified physician. Yet for all my personal blessings, my American dream is incomplete. When I look around my immediate environment, it's rare for me to see anyone who looks like me. Most days, I don't see anyone whom I can relate to on these very personal, foundational levels, and more importantly, my children don't either. Instead, as I take my early-morning jogs through my neighborhood of four-thousand-square-foot homes and well-manicured lawns, I'm occasionally met with the same suspicion that George Zimmerman had of Trayvon Martin.[9]

What does being a man of African descent in my neighborhood tell me? It reveals the underlying truth of the American dream—that the dream was never meant for people who look like me. I am an exception, the man who achieved this dream even though I was never welcomed into it. If I have anything to say about it, my children will be part of a larger, more inclusive, American dream.

I am writing this now so that I can leave somewhat of a legacy to my three beautiful children; I hope my story will serve as a motivator during whatever trials and tribulations they may have in their own lives' journeys. To my children Gabrielle, Vivienne, and Kingston, I want you all to be proud of who you are and where you come from, no matter what. You will encounter people in your life who will tell you that you cannot achieve your goals and, worse still, will assume that such ambitions aren't yours to pursue. These people will not know you. They will not know your strength, your drive, or your history. Always stand true to your convictions, remain firm in your character, be peaceful in your heart, and be thankful for God's presence in your life. Last but not least, place no limitations on whatever it is you want to do in life. Your individual journeys will be different from mine, of course, but in the larger sense, your paths will not be dissimilar from those in the pages you are about to read. And as you read my story, I hope you will get a sense of why your father is who he is, and you will remember that a piece of him is in your genetic makeup. In your veins runs the blood of people who persevere and are resilient in the face of all obstacles. I can only pray that one day these words will touch each of your souls and make you better children, siblings, future parents and, ultimately, more loving, compassionate human beings.

---

9 Visit the website of the *Washington Post* at http://www.washingtonpost.com/opinions/to-be-black-in america-/2012/03/22/gIQAEKr4TS_story.html?utm_term=.5f2941388662 for more information.

CHAPTER 10

Ancestors and Origins—What's in a Name?

IN ORDER TO TELL MY story, I must begin with those who came before me. My mother and father, who each played an integral role in shaping my life, were both immigrants; they came to this country from Haiti in the mid-1970s. In order to understand me, you must understand them too.

My father, Serge Madhere, was born in 1950. He was one of seven children who hailed from a relatively secluded town in Haiti called Baradères. His own mother had died in childbirth when delivering one of his younger siblings, and so from the age of eight, he was raised by my grandfather, Exuma Madhere—also known as Papy—and my great-grandmother, Elina Madhere, whom we called our grand-mère. My father grew up watching his father provide for his entire family on a skilled laborer's salary. Raising seven children on such a tight income required many sacrifices on my grandfather's part, and it was this spirit of generosity, along with my grandfather's work ethic, that shaped my father most deeply. In addition to my father's natural, God-given abilities, this work ethic—which he would later pass on to my brother and me—placed my father at the top of his academic class in grade school.

In high school, my father excelled in his classes and developed a fine passion for Haitian history, the arts, and poetry. He began writing poems and parables, which quickly became popular among Haiti's various disenfranchised populations. His work became so well known that his writings caught the attention of François "Papa Doc" Duvalier, Haiti's dictator. Duvalier branded my father as an "intellectual." Under Papa Doc, an intellectual was nearly tantamount to being an enemy of the regime. Anyone who spoke about the tactics of the government's repression, including some clergymen who were my father's grammar school teachers, were faced with the fear of exile or execution.

My father's writings and academic success ultimately landed him acceptance into France's Paris-Sorbonne University, a premier European university. There were a number of reasons that led my father to pursue his education in Paris, but Papa Doc's persecution was first and foremost among them. As a "known intellectual"—that is, someone who was educated and intelligent enough to potentially challenge Duvalier's "President for Life" title—my father was a viable target for Duvalier's ruthless paramilitary army, best known today as the Tonton Macoutes. In fact, many people today believe that many of Haiti's current socioeconomic problems are a direct result of Duvalier's forced mass exodus of brilliant minds out of the country.[10]

While in France, my father faced discrimination from his professors and was isolated socially because of his Haitian descent. This was a consequence of both inherent racism and the centuries-old tenuous relationship between Haiti and France. His own father had to support a family of six on a laborer's salary, so he could not send money to help my father through school. Since Paris was not very friendly to black immigrants, my father struggled to find work and pay for food and other things he needed. When I was a child, my dad often told me that his circumstances in Paris were so atrocious that he became malnourished. His condition got so bad that when his sister visited, she wept upon seeing him. Malnutrition had caused patches of his hair to fall out. However, my father's inner drive and strength, fueled by his own father's example of grit and determination, allowed him to persevere. My dad told me that this particular time in his life built so much character and confidence in him that he felt he could be dropped off anywhere in the world with fifty dollars in his pocket, and he would find a way to succeed.

---

10 Supporting information about François Duvalier's regime can be found by visiting the archives of the *New York Times* at http://www.nytimes.com/1971/04/23/archives/papa-doc-a-ruthless-dictator-kept-the-haitians-in-illiteracy-and.html.

My mother, Marie I. Magaly Jacques, was born in November 1953 into very different circumstances from my father. Her father (my grandfather, Gerard Jacques) was a proud man who worked as a high-level accountant for Haiti's Port Authority. He married my grandmother, Francesca Jacques, a peaceful, mild-mannered woman who exemplified strong Christian values that she passed on to her children. My maternal grandparents stressed the importance of high personal achievement, strong family values, and global citizenship. These values, along with my grandfather's government job, allowed my mother to live a relatively sheltered, upper-middle-class lifestyle.

My parents eventually met at a party organized by their two schools. Their attraction was instantaneous. In a world without social media and cell phones, they would intermittently lose contact with each other, but fate led them to meet again three days prior to my father's leaving for college. Although they were facing years apart, my parents' love was so strong that neither was deterred. When my father graduated in 1975, they were married immediately and settled in Brooklyn, New York. By 1977, my older brother (also named Serge) was born, and with my arrival on October 16, 1980, we became a family of four.

I can only imagine what these early years in America were like for my parents. In my own life today, I realize how challenging changes can be. Starting a new job, changing schools, moving homes, or even something as mundane as a shift in my daily routine can be chaotic and frightening. Yet my parents had to face these challenges—and many, many more—as immigrants and young parents. It must have been so difficult for them to navigate daily life while becoming accustomed to an entirely new culture and mastering a new language. I try to understand how they balanced their new American identity with their strong cultural roots. I think of my dad, who grew up as a poor child in this hemisphere's poorest country, who never lost his deep and abiding love for Haiti. Did leaving his country for higher pursuits afflict his soul? Did his dedication to helping his homeland get thrown off course when my brother and I were born, or did he always plan on having children? How did my mother, with the values and morals her parents taught her, fully maintain her identity and self-worth while raising children in this foreign land? And through all this, how did my parents manage to instill such strong values in my brother and me?

My name, Maxime, is the creation of my mother's heart and imagination. She penned this acrostic poem just after I was born:

> **M**ade of beautiful gold laced with silk
> **A**t dawn on a Wednesday morning
> **X**anthic in color with golden hair
> **I**n came my baby boy;
> **M**y heart almost broke in shock
> "**E**nough!" I said. I accept this gift from God!

As a child, I didn't appreciate my name. It was so often mispronounced that it became a constant source of anxiety for me. In English, the *e* at the end of my name is silent, making the proper pronunciation "Maxim," but having such an unusual, decisively un-American name led to all manner of incorrect variations.

My mother shared this poem with me on the day I asked why she had given me such an odd name. It wasn't until much later in life that I realized my name's true value. Although my parents were rapidly assimilating into American culture, my name—and my brother's name too—served as badges to express my parents' nationalistic pride. (My father had also had a teacher by the name of Maxime—that had been the crowning point on their decision.) Although my parents came to America for the safety and opportunities it offered, they wanted us to love our Haitian heritage. Beyond that, they wanted to free their children of the burdens many black Americans carry from being born into a country where they have been an oppressed minority.

Yet, I almost did not have my name, at least if the county clerk had gotten her way. When my mother went to register my birth certificate, the clerk, an African American woman, challenged the spelling. She told my mother that the *e* in *Maxime* made my name look feminine and that other children would tease me. "This is America, not Haiti," she told my mother.

My mother, in her strength and pride, would have none of it. She explained to the clerk that I was named after the Holy Roman Emperor Maximilian, and the root of my name came from the Latin word meaning "special." The clerk quickly lost interest, but my mother knew that my name, and my heritage, would link me to a country of black people who overthrew their enslavers, becoming the only nation of slaves ever to do so. She believed my name would imbue me with strength and a connection to a culture that so many people of African descent in this country have had stolen from them. Through no fault of their own, that part of their story was stripped by European slave traders and suppressed during the Jim Crow era.

Armed with the knowledge that I came from a people who had successfully overthrown their enslavers, as I matured, so did my appreciation for my name. Thus, when my grandfather used to tell me the old proverb, "Until lions have their historians, tales of the hunt shall always glorify the hunter," nowhere was this more evident than in the thought process my mother must have had when she chose my name. Because my family had our cultural identity, because we knew our roots and the values against which we should measure ourselves, my mother knew that my brother and I would always carry with us the strength of our origins.

CHAPTER 11

A Family Divided

As does so much of my life, my first clear memory deals with race. People of African descent in America are inherently separated. The color of our skin, the texture of our hair, the diction of our speech, and so many other factors make us "others" in our own country. Young children pick up on this all too quickly, and although Serge couldn't have realized it, by the time he was five or six years old, he'd incorporated this "otherness" into his psyche. He didn't mean any harm, of course, but this led to his twisting of what is a common, innocent-enough joke into a race-based trick—a trick that I remember to this day.

I was about three years old and enrolled in day care. When my mother came to bring me home at the end of the day, I ran into her arms with all the elation of a young child. As I gathered up my things, my friend—a white boy whom I'd spent the afternoon playing with—asked me about the woman who was picking me up. When I explained that she was my mother, my young, confused friend cried, "But she's black; you're orange!" I remember looking down at my own skin but largely ignoring his comment. But later that evening, I asked Serge about the incident. He told me, "You *are* orange. Mom and Dad aren't your real parents—that's why you don't look like us. You were adopted."

I didn't know the definition of *adopted*, but my young mind clearly understood that I was being marked as different. I cried so hard that night. When my parents learned what Serge had done, he was punished severely. Unfortunately for me, the damage had already been done. I was now different in some fundamental way because of my skin. Little did I know then that this would be a defining element throughout my life.

The year was 1984. I had just woken up from a deep sleep in my father's used Nissan Sentra. Serge was sitting next to me in the back seat. It was pitch dark outside, and I was trying to focus my tired eyes to figure out what was going on. I realized that I wasn't in my own bed, as was the case when I initially fell asleep that night. I noticed that my dad was in the driver's seat, but the front passenger's seat was empty. "Daddy, where are we going? Where's Mommy?" I asked. My father had responded that we were going to uncle Paul and Tatie Parnelle's house for a visit. I happily said, "We are having a sleepover at our cousin's house!" My dad remained silent.

Uncle Paul and Tatie Parnelle had a large home with a huge backyard where Serge and I would play with our cousins, JanPol and Rodney, for hours. At the time, I didn't think anything was unusual about our trip. Uncle Paul was best friends with my father, and Tatie Parnelle was my mother's cousin. They always made us feel welcome in their home, and on this visit, my uncle told Serge and me warmly, "This is the room you will stay in. Go ahead and make yourselves comfortable." I remember arriving at their house with a lot of suitcases. I had no idea that we were not just visiting but there to stay. My parents were divorcing.

Despite my parents' deep and abiding love for each other, and despite their having eked out an appreciable measure of success here in America, my parents divorced when I was four years old. My mother, unfortunately, battled depression and bipolar disorder, and eventually, the point came when it was healthier for them to separate. I didn't know what divorce was at that time, of course, but my life—formerly centered around our Canarsie neighborhood—now became split between my mother's new neighborhood in Brownsville and Hempstead in Long Island.

The initial effects of the separation were immediately felt, at least in the fiscal sense. Prior to their breakup, my parents had bought a house together in

Long Island, but the stress and abruptness of the divorce forced them to sell the house at a financial loss because neither could afford the mortgage payments on their own. Trying to give my brother and me a sense of normalcy while their own worlds were crumbling, my parents wanted us to stay with my uncle and Tatie Parnelle until my father could get back on his feet financially. Dad was a new PhD graduate who wasn't making much money at the time. Mom was in a similar circumstance, as she was trying to put her life back together while going to school and dealing with her mental illness.

Looking back on it, staying at my uncle Paul's probably helped lay, in a formative way, my first inclination toward medicine. Uncle Paul was an internist with a specialization in gastroenterology. The fruits of his success were easy for me to recognize, even at such a young age. His sprawling home was vastly different from our cramped apartment, and his Long Island neighborhood was a world apart from my ultra-urban, poor-and-working-class environment in Brooklyn. Having a "second father" who was dedicated to both his career and family provided me with an invaluable model of adulthood and a glimpse of who I could become.

At first, living at my aunt and uncle's house didn't bother me much. I liked it there, and I had fun with my cousins. But within a week or two, I realized someone was missing: my mother. I remember crying to Tatie Parnelle often, asking for my mother. Her response was always the same: "Mommy's at work, but you will see her this weekend." When Fridays would finally come, my father, despite the long hours he worked, would drive us to Brooklyn without fail. This became our new routine: weekdays and school on Long Island with my father, weekends in Brooklyn with my mother.

Upon further reflection, I wonder how many times I asked Tatie Parnelle, or my father, "Where's Mommy?" I pestered my mom with questions, too, repeatedly asking, "Mommy, why are you always crying?" and "Why can't you stay with us?" I did not understand how much my questions must have pained her, and she would always appear as if she was holding back tears. I think of the predicament my questioning placed them in. How often did the adults in my life need to craft a response without overtly lying or hurting my young feelings? Children are naturally inquisitive. How did it feel when I asked them—innocently enough but probably with all the bluntness of a child—these heavy, emotionally laden questions?

My young self didn't realize just how much had changed in my family until one weekend when Serge and I were ill. We must have had the flu or a bad cold because I remember my mother making soup for us throughout the weekend. When Sunday night came, my mother announced that my father was on his way to pick us up. She got our coats.

I didn't want to go. I was a young child, sick, and I wanted my mother. I complained that my throat hurt, but my mother insisted that Serge and I had to go back to Long Island. Despite my pleas, my mother continued to get me ready for the forty-five-minute ride back to Hempstead. I was hurt—why was she ignoring me? Serge understood about their divorce, but I didn't. All I knew was that I wanted to stay. I wanted my mom.

My mother began buttoning up my coat. I protested that it was too tight, but she insisted that I bundle up because it was cold outside, and my father would arrive at any minute. When the doorbell rang, she rushed to let my father in. Usually, when my father arrived, Serge and I would be waiting on the sofa eagerly and obediently, with our schoolbags packed. But not this day. My mother explained that we were both sick and were still getting ready. My father was not happy. Serge was on his way out of the bedroom when we heard our father's booming, Haitian-accented voice yell, "Serge, Max, let's go!"

Serge, who was seven years old at the time, was always the more mischievous sibling, so he got into more trouble and knew what Dad's punishments were like. He warned me that I didn't want to see Dad upset, saying I'd receive a spanking. Yet my young, fragile mind couldn't conceptualize what was going on. As we came out of the bedroom to meet my father, he demanded to know where my coat was. My response was simple: "Daddy, I'm sick. Serge is sick too. We should all stay here, just the four of us, like we used to."

My father demanded that I get ready, but I refused. This stalemate went on for several minutes before, in my stubbornness and desperation, I talked back, which is a particularly serious offense in Haitian culture. "No!" I yelled. "I'm staying with my mommy!" I'd barely finished my sentence when my father hit me on my buttocks so hard with his open hand that I remember the force of the strike to this day. This was the moment of truth about the new dynamics of our family, brought to the forefront by a four-year-old's tantrum. My parents were divorced: it would never be just the four of us again.

In the meltdown that followed, I remember looking into the eyes of my parents. Thinking back on it now, their looks were of sadness, pain, anger, and regret. Regret that even though they had created a new life for themselves in this new country, the realities of that life had driven a wedge into their young family. Regret, also, that the consequences of those decisions were to be played out in front of them by the trajectories of the two children they had conceived together.

A divorce, no matter how amicable, always affects children in subconscious ways. In my case, the two lives I was living—between Hempstead in Long Island and Brownsville in Brooklyn—were two very different experiences. Yet both of those lives were filled with love, protection, and my parents' determination to provide the very best they could for Serge and me.

My father had earned his doctorate in statistics and psychometrics in 1981. He taught us to value education, yet our grades in school were never particularly good. Perhaps this was an effect of the divorce itself or of moving between Hempstead and Brownsville each week; I am not sure. Yet despite our grades, my father always encouraged our individuality and fostered our innate talents. In first grade, after yet another lukewarm report card, my father took me along to a parent–teacher conference with my teacher. Not only did my teacher call into question my intelligence, but he also told my father that I likely had some form of attention deficit disorder. While it was true that I had some trouble staying on task—my daydreaming often led to penalties for incomplete assignments—I remember my father's response to my teacher clearly. "This boy comes from a family of freethinkers and poets. If you think that is daydreaming, then let him dream!" To my father, hindering my creativity would only block my chances of success later in life. More importantly, my father didn't want me to potentially be placed on a special education pathway because of "daydreaming." At the time, he was actually doing research on cultural models of intelligence; he later published a paper on this very topic. In my particular circumstance, he thought that the teacher was displaying cultural bias, and he didn't want me to have the stigma of "learning disability" attached to my profile.

My career at that particular school ended shortly because my father, believing my teacher was discriminating against me because I was a black boy in a majority-white suburban school, pulled me out. Our new school must've suited us better because I don't remember having many academic issues. I do remember the school being more diverse even though I didn't have many friends—most of my friends remained those from my local neighborhood. However, it was during these years that my neighborhood imparted my "second" education.

Our section of Hempstead was an upward-mobility area where many middle-class black people had moved their families in an attempt to distance themselves from the problems of the inner cities. Unfortunately, some of these problems will always find their way into the suburbs, and this was true in Hempstead.

In the afternoons, after our homework was done (which was *a must* in our household), Serge and I would play football with the other kids in the neighborhood. One of our closer friends, Drew, came over to our house almost every day. Drew's father had died, and his mother worked long hours, leaving him unsupervised after school. Drew stayed at our house so often that my father told him one afternoon, "From now on, before you go outside and play with my boys, I expect to see all of your completed homework."

My father was kind to Drew and often invited him to stay for dinner. But at the same time, Dad knew that Drew's home life was unstable. Drew naturally had all the traits of a leader, but his lack of supervision concerned my father—he knew that without a strong parental presence, young people can stray down some destructive paths.

My father sat both Serge and me down at the dinner table one evening. He told us that while he liked Drew, we had to be careful not to follow his every action. He reminded us that we were raised to be individuals—not followers—and cautioned us to always listen to our gut. "If you even have to question a choice, then most likely you know it's something I wouldn't approve of. There's only one leader in this house, and that is Daddy."

Serge and I didn't fully understand at the time, but we did know the consequences of not listening to our father. We continued to play football with Drew, but we were careful to keep our distance when he was hanging out with the neighborhood's older boys. However, one day after Drew interrupted our football game to go talk with the older kids, I decided to watch him from a distance, just to see what was going on. As he talked, I saw one of his friends hand him a crumpled-up brown paper bag, which Drew then slid into his backpack.

When I later asked Drew what was in the bag, he told me that he didn't really know but that "some of the older white boys buy this shit up!" before adding that he wouldn't be dealing much longer. His goal was to buy a motorbike and be "the flyest kid in Hempstead." He also warned me not to tell my father, knowing my dad would rain down punishment on us both if he found out. Even though I didn't tell on Drew, the high standards my dad held me to helped me make sound, reasonable decisions in Hempstead—and throughout my entire life—and so I began distancing myself from my friend even further.

Soon enough, Drew got his motorbike. He stopped playing football entirely and instead spent the afternoons speeding through the neighborhood. When my father found out about Drew's motorbike, we were forbidden from hanging out with him. However, this didn't prevent my brother and me from running to the window to watch Drew put on a show each evening as the streetlights came on, as if he were the neighborhood rock star. Dad joined us one evening. As we watched, my father shook his head in disbelief. "I'm afraid for this boy," he said with a sigh.

While Serge and I didn't always agree with our father, we respected and obeyed him, and unfortunately, in Drew's case, Dad was right to worry. Drew was killed in a collision later that year. When he passed, I was filled with regret. Young as I was, some part of me knew that Drew's recklessness stemmed from the instability in his home. Without a strong parental presence, he'd followed the path of many young, black, urban males and looked for validation on the streets. As I matured into my early adult years, I would sometimes think of Drew and wonder how many young men of African descent we have lost to either an early death or the criminal justice system. With Drew's inherent drive and leadership, he could have gone on to do great things if his best qualities had been cultivated and reinforced in his environment. How many other young men have we lost so needlessly?

My weekends with my mother were very different from our weekdays in Hempstead, but my mother, too, was dedicated to raising us well, teaching us to value education and shielding us from life's harsher realities.

Our Brownsville neighborhood was a historically troubled area to which low-income minorities had flocked during the 1960s and 1970s after the city began building public housing in the neighborhood. Yet as rough as Brownsville was, the bordering neighborhood, Brooklyn's East New York, was even rougher. By the time the crack epidemic of the 1980s came along, East New York was one of the most drug-ridden areas in New York City, and the boundaries between Brownsville and East New York were blurring.

One of my most vivid memories from Brownsville is also one of the most tragic I've ever witnessed. A young black man, who couldn't have been more than twenty years old, was shot in front of our apartment building. As we approached our building, my mother tried to whisk Serge and me upstairs quickly, but there was no hiding what had happened. I watched in horror as the paramedics tried to resuscitate the young man. This was my first encounter with death. The image of this man dead on the pavement, with the police and paramedics swarming around him, was immediately burned into my seven-year-old mind. It remains there to this day.

As I reflect, I realize how many of the elements that plague our inner cities were a part of our Brownsville weekend experiences. Drugs, junkies, prostitution, violence, dirty streets and parks, homelessness, domestic abuse, welfare dependence, and many other aspects endemic to high-poverty areas were so ingrained in the landscape that this had all become normalized for the area's residents. Serge and I did have the alternate experience of Hempstead to contrast Brownsville against, but on some level, this way of life was normalized for us too.

Our Brownsville apartment was on Church Avenue, on the eleventh floor of a housing development. My mother did her best to shield us from as much of the world below as she could. She always managed to put a positive spin on everything, explaining societal ills in a way that eased and placated our young minds. The loud gunshots that would routinely wake us from our sleep were merely "people playing with firecrackers." The empty crack vials discarded in our hallways were never drug paraphernalia, only "broken pieces of glass and furniture." Arguing neighbors and the domestic violence that often ensued became "adults playing around, just like you and Serge." Even when we heard or saw police sirens, my mom would simply say, "Those are our neighborhood watchers, making sure we are safe." How a woman struggling against depression found a way to paint our lives in Brownsville in such a positive light is a testament to her dedication as a parent and her own inner strength.

When my mother couldn't shield us, she did her best to turn the neighborhood's ills into teaching moments. If we were on our way to early-morning Sunday school and saw scantily clad prostitutes returning home after a long night, she would say that the women had been out partying and making "poor decisions." If we asked why the junkie passed out in front of our building didn't have parents to care for him or clean clothes to wear, she would explain that a solid education could help us from finding ourselves in a predicament like his. "That is part of the reason your father and I work very hard to provide you with whatever you need to do well in school," she would tell us.

Regardless of how hard my mom worked to shelter us, there was only so much she could do. Brownsville was a reflection of many poor, inner-city communities all over America, replete with the problems of America's toughest urban neighborhoods. As hard as she tried, my mother simply couldn't be with us every moment of every weekend. When mom wasn't around, Serge and I would spend much of our time at a local park. Outside of sports, much of our play involved fighting. Roughhousing was common, but so were serious fights. Fighting was a response to our environment—we needed to be tough. Emulating this behavior seemed natural to us. It was simply a way of life in Brownsville. As young black children, we had to adapt to our surroundings, or we risked becoming easy targets. As we grew, Serge and I became tougher, more resilient, and more "street," not necessarily because we wanted to, but because we *had* to.

We didn't bring this behavior home, of course. Neither of our parents would ever have tolerated it. In Brownsville, my mother reminded us every single weekend of the consequences of poor decision-making, and even as she drilled the value of education into our heads, I also often heard my father's critical commentaries in my mind, which urged me to follow my gut. So, even though Serge and I were raised in two very different environments, my parents' strength, morals, and direction sang as one in my mind.

As an adult, I've come to understand that my parents' explanations of Brownsville were overly simplistic, perhaps even crass, in a way. Most of the families in Brownsville didn't choose poverty. Some had lived in poverty for so many generations that any other way of living had essentially become both inconceivable and unattainable. Yet poverty, in and of itself, is not a mark of immorality. There are good, kindhearted, God-fearing people trying to provide for their families within any economic spectrum. Unfortunately, once a cycle of poverty has begun, it is extremely difficult to escape—especially in neighborhoods like Brownsville, where temptations and distractions lurk on every corner. Yet, thanks largely to my father's own experiences with poverty in Haiti, my parents were able to teach me how to use my experiences in Brownsville as something that humbled and motivated me simultaneously. Despite our circumstances, Serge and I were never made to feel that Brownsville's poverty was our only possible fate. Yes, we knew we had to be "street" outside the home as a matter of safety, but we also knew that there was a world of possibilities beyond those streets. We were raised to expect that our lives would have choices.

In 1988, my parents decided that it was time for us to see their homeland. We spent that summer, along with our cousins, at my maternal grandparents' house in Port-au-Prince, Haiti. My grandparents didn't speak much English—none at all, really—but Serge and I picked up a working knowledge of Kreyòl quickly enough. I remember having a wonderful summer. My grandfather's government job allowed my grandparents to live very comfortably. In their neighborhood, which was set high on the hill above the main city, my grandparents had a nice house with a pool in the backyard, a small farm with chickens for us to chase, and a maid who cooked all three meals each day. My grandparents lived close to a beach, which we visited several times a week. The local fishermen would take us out on their boats, and we'd help them haul in fish, conch, and lobster.

During that summer, my mom took us to many historical sites, where we learned about François-Dominique Toussaint Louverture, the great leader of the Haitian revolution; Jean-Jacques Dessalines, the first ruler of Haiti under its 1801 constitution; and others who helped our people throw off the chains of bondage and revolt against France. We also visited *Le Negre Marron* (*The Black Maroon*, sometimes also translated as *The Unknown Slave*), a statue depicting a man who escaped slavery—with his clearly broken bonds—lifting a conch shell to his lips. The statue, a symbol of freedom and power, stands in front of Haiti's presidential palace. *Le Negre Marron* left such an indelible mark on me that I have a painting of it in my house to this day.

Unlike in America, where most paintings and statues of "great men" depict white Europeans, in Haiti, I found a whole world of respected, revered men who looked like me, who looked like a man I could become. How deeply did seeing myself represented in Haiti's history shape my young mind? Certainly, this isn't something I can quantify, but the effect of inclusion and representation in such a fundamental way is always profound.

That summer, we also visited my paternal family. While Papy Madhere's home, which he still shared with my great-grandmother Elina, was more modest than that of my mother's parents, I took great pride in knowing that they lived around the corner from the presidential palace.

Grand-mère Elina cooked us a great feast when we arrived. Her table was replete with *lanbi* (conch), *woma boukannen* (grilled lobster), *bannann* (plantains), and *diri* (rice). Throughout our visit, Grand-mère told us many stories about my father as a child, and I listened as my grandfather Papy proudly recounted how he, a "little old craftsman from Baradères," created a better life for himself and his large family in Port-au-Prince, despite the odds.

Of all the things my father's family imparted to me during my visit, something Grand-mère told me and my brother still sticks with me. She said that our father had succeeded beyond Papy's accomplishments and that Papy had succeeded beyond his own father. Therefore, it was our job to exceed the accomplishments of our own mother and father. A rough translation of what she said is, "If the children do not exceed their parents, there has been no progress made in the family."

Now that I'm a parent with children of my own, the words of my great-grandmother are all the more poignant. Not only do I want the best for my children so that they can grow up to be compassionate, upstanding individuals, but I also want to give them the very best education possible—and not necessarily because advanced degrees often equate to high salaries. Education sharpens the mind, exposes us to new ideas, and teaches us to think critically and make informed choices. Education provides options; the more options my children have, the greater their chances of leading fulfilling, successful, lives.

My first trip to Haiti was perhaps not as idyllic as I've made it sound. Serge and I witnessed almost unimaginable poverty during our trip—poverty far greater and more systemic than anything we'd seen in Brooklyn. Children younger than I walked the streets barefoot, often searching for food in the trash; we saw entire communities of tin-constructed homes with straw-thatched roofs; piles of garbage a full story high lined many streets; and many corners were home to beggars who were so emaciated that they lacked even the drive to beg. Many homes in Port-au-Prince lacked (and still lack, as of this writing) even basic plumbing: human body odor strong enough to pierce my nostrils wasn't uncommon.

Thus, I left Haiti with mixed emotions. On the one hand, I enjoyed spending time with my parents' families, and I found it fascinating to see the land where my parents had been raised—a land I'd been taught to respect. Yet on the other hand, Haiti taught me how fortunate I truly was; I thanked God I was born in a place where I didn't have to endure such hardship and poverty. At eight years old, most children in developed countries are concerned with toys, fun, and games, yet my trip to Haiti taught me humility.

My visit to Haiti served as a milestone in my life. It was the first time I learned—through firsthand experience—not to take anything for granted. Whether or not teaching me this lesson was a part of my parents' intention is debatable, but this is definitely how I processed that first experience visiting our homeland. Coming back to America, I promised myself that I would never take any opportunity for granted. In the years to come, that promise would compel me in many ways.

When we returned from Haiti, I learned that my life was in for a big change. Even as we were recounting our trip, I could see the glee on my father's face—he had good news to tell us. He'd been offered a position at Howard University in Washington, DC. "This is something that I want to do," he told us, "but if you don't want to come with me, then I am not going. I love you guys too much."

My young mind knew very little about DC, other than that the president lived there. When I asked how far away Washington was, the long look on Serge's face told me everything I needed to know: DC was far. My father told me DC was about a four-hour drive from home before explaining why he thought it was a good idea to move. For one thing, he wanted to distance us from Brownsville's less desirable elements. Just as importantly, we were in a predominately white school, and my parents didn't want cultural bias to play any role in determining our early education outcomes. We also found it hard to focus with everything going on in our personal lives. I can vividly remember staying up late at night in my bed, trying to strategize how I was going to bring my family back together. Our grades reflected such inner turmoil, and we performed poorly in school. Our father felt our split environment was responsible for a large part of our anemic grades.

Moving to a new place seemed exciting, especially to a city like DC, which I'd seen on TV. Serge immediately understood the move to mean more time and distance away from our mother, but I was too young to grasp such a simple concept. My imagination only pictured a new place to live, a bigger house, and new friends. I thought about the places I'd seen on TV, like the White House, the Washington Monument, and the Lincoln Memorial. I didn't stop to consider what I'd be missing: the genuine compassion, support, and forgiveness that only a mother can give a child.

When my dad proposed the move, I can only imagine the fear and trepidation the distance must have inspired in my mother. Would the unconditional love we had for her somehow be lessened if she weren't around as often? Would she be able to be a part of all our important milestones? Would my father find a new wife, someone who could take her place in our hearts? Would we resent her or think she'd abandoned us? And who would care for us when we were sick?

As much as my mother loved us, she understood that she'd never be able to provide us with one key aspect—our father. She firmly believed that my father would teach her young boys to become *men.* She'd seen too many boys in Brownsville without a father or strong male role model in their lives. She didn't want that for us. Swallowing her pride and the expectation of what a mother "should" be, my mom trusted in God that she was doing the right thing.

From that time on, the bond between my mother and I grew even stronger. Although we were separated by distance, there was hardly ever a day when we didn't speak. No topics were off-limits, and we became best friends. I've never made a decision, faced a challenge, or celebrated a moment in my life without her.

CHAPTER 12

Life in the Chocolate City (Washington, DC)

MY FATHER'S NEW JOB LED us to a new life. We lived in Takoma Park, an upper-middle-class, majority–African American neighborhood with tree-lined streets. In this neighborhood, everyone looked like me, and everyone was successful like my father. I had no issues fitting in, and I never felt like a minority because we were the area's majority, in terms of both race and class. Seeing black success during my preteen and teenage years became normal for me.

My father taught statistics at Howard University, a nationally ranked historically black college and university (HBCU), and most of his students and co-faculty were African American. One of my father's main interests was black liberation. He would frequently come home with books on African American history. Our home-video collection consisted largely of movies depicting the African American experience. *Eyes on the Prize*, a fourteen-part documentary about America's Civil Rights Movement, and *Roots*, the seminal 1977 miniseries based on Alex Haley's novel, which chronicled the lives of an African American family from slavery in colonial America through to the Civil War era, are among the videos I remember best. The first full-length book I remember reading in its entirety was the *Autobiography of Malcolm X*. The evolution of Malcolm X's thoughts and beliefs throughout his lifetime, despite his humble beginnings, left a deep impression on me.

Why are these worth mentioning? Because my father's books and videos imbued in me a sense of personal responsibility. Watching children no older than myself being attacked by police dogs or having hoses turned on them during a basic human rights protest was—simply put—mind-blowing. It made me reflect on blackness itself, on what it meant to have skin this color. On my trip to Haiti, I'd learned about the revolt and violence from which my country was born, and now I saw African Americans enduring similar violence. If being born black was such a tremendous "burden" that our ancestors had to fight torture and rape and bondage just to gain a measure of equality, then who was I to take their struggles for granted? Who was I to deny the opportunities now offered to me? These were people who had fought for my right to sit at a desk in school and learn my lessons, and—with this knowledge now pressed into my psyche—it became much easier for me to focus on my work and do whatever my teacher asked of me.

From simply staying on task, my grades in middle school began to improve. In particular, my sixth-grade teachers, Ms. Tierney and Mr. Seldon, saw a potential in me that I couldn't yet see for myself, and they encouraged and guided me as I began to focus more seriously on my studies. Before I knew it, I was starting to be labeled the "smart" kid. The label didn't make me feel any more special, but the joy that bringing home straight-A report cards brought to my parents made a huge difference in my self-esteem. Plus, anytime I did well, my dad would give me $100, as well as a trip to a restaurant of my choosing where I could order whatever I liked from the menu. By the time I reached eighth grade, my teacher, Ms. Weaver, was determined that I begin my high school career as fully prepared and academically engaged as possible. She pushed me in ways that only made me strive harder.

Of course, being labeled in school as the smart kid had its negatives as well. Joe, my middle school's resident quintessential bully, tried to teach me about these negatives. One afternoon, after he'd heard that I'd gotten a straight-A report card, Joe decided to "test" me himself. We had just finished a classroom assignment, and as I was walking toward the front of the classroom to turn it in, Joe yanked my paper out of my hand and stomped on it. He called me a bitch. I shouted back at him. Then he delivered a right hook to my face, a punch hard enough to knock me to the ground. Blind fury overtook me. I unleashed all I had on Joe. By the time I had calmed myself down, the whole classroom was cheering for me—I'd gotten the best of the bully.

Fortunately for me, I never had to deal with bullying in middle school again. Unfortunately for many young black men across America, particularly in urban environments, there's always a "Joe" to obstruct educational pursuits. "Joe" doesn't have to be a person, per se, "Joe" can be any form of disruption—gangs, drugs, poverty, neglect, an abusive parent, or an unequal educational system. For the child who cannot defend against such "Joes," for the student who is expected to fail, how does that child shape a positive self-identity? How is he or she supposed to understand his or her own potential? The answer, too often, is that the child instead falls victim to the toxic environment. But can you blame that child for becoming a product of toxicity? Although I am far from perfect, I have been blessed with strong parents, a strong cultural heritage, and with the self-pride and self-esteem that stem from these blessings. I will try to teach these values to my children as they make their way through their own educational careers.

There weren't many viable public school options in DC, as far as my father was concerned. Even though there were good private schools in the area, my father didn't have the financial means to send me or my brother to these schools. However, one afternoon, a local private school sent representatives to my middle school to recruit minority students. The reps were from a well-respected institution—members of Congress, high-ranking government officials, and other elite professionals enrolled their children there.

My high grades caught the attention of these recruiters. I remember being removed, along with two of my friends, from my eighth-grade English class to meet with one of the recruiters. As the three of us entered the interview room, I overheard the recruiter explain to my principal, "We only want your brightest African American boys." The recruiter then proceeded to pitch to us the school's many amenities, including the sprawling campus, an Olympic-sized pool, a basketball court, a state-of-the-art football field, and a soccer stadium. Conspicuously absent, however, was any real mention of academics. At the end of the presentation, we were invited to an open house the following weekend.

When I went home that day, I told my father about the meeting. He congratulated me on being one of the very few selected from my school, and he reminded me that doing well in school would continue to pay off in the future. When we arrived at the open house that weekend, we were first taken to the auditorium, where multiple speakers talked about their experiences. Each speaker focused on camaraderie and fond memories but glanced over academics. We were then taken to the football and soccer fields, where we met the coaches. On our tour of the basketball court, the tour guide exclaimed that he was looking forward to the day when we would win another championship banner for the school.

By that point, my dad had had enough. He resoundingly told the tour guide that if he sent me to this institution, it wouldn't be with the purpose of winning championships and adding glory to the school. He then asked, quite firmly, that we be taken on a tour of the classrooms so that we could meet the teachers. Lastly, he demanded that we be allowed to meet other students of African descent so that we could get a feeling for what the school was *really* like.

The tour guide, made beet red by my father's words, replied that the classrooms were next on the tour. We were taken to the English teacher's classroom. The teacher, a white male, didn't focus on academics but instead talked at length about the number of lobbyists, senators, and other successful people who had sat in his classroom. In the middle of this diatribe, my father interrupted, "Sir, I am not here to listen to how many members of Congress have matriculated from this school. I am here to find out about the success rates of your minority students! Now, where are your minority students?" The teacher's answer was quite astonishing, and even I, at thirteen years old, knew it smacked of racism. "It's a weekend," he replied. "Our basketball and football teams have road games today."

My father was about to explode when in walked an African American alumnus. He was a soft-spoken young man who had recently graduated from college. He explained that he had enjoyed his high school years, saying that he would do it all over again. He then boasted that he was a part of the school's large and well-connected local alumni community and that he was now serving as one of the school's dorm masters.

We left immediately. When we got into the car, my dad said firmly, "Max, you are not going to this school. They have no intention of cultivating your mind." I was upset, but my father went on to explain that this school wasn't interested in me academically—they only saw me as someone who would fit the black athlete stereotype. He explained no one at this school would ever truly see me as an individual, that I'd only be a poster boy for their minority recruitment efforts. "If the best minority representative they have for open-house day is merely a *dorm master*, this is not the place for us," he said.

I'll never forget those words. My dad was right. Impressionable minds can get caught up by superficial and trivial things, and I was certainly mesmerized. I was enamored with the school's facilities, the amenities, and the famous alumni, but I never stopped to consider the dearth of successful alumni who looked like me. My father knew—as I now understand as a father—that raising a child of color in a world full of stereotypes is no easy task. He understood how the media glorifies only those black Americans who fit into specific tropes—the athlete, the entertainer, the rapper—too many of whom lead sensationalistic lifestyles not befitting true role models. Black professionals, politicians, and entrepreneurs are largely left out of the picture, and in turn, the "real world" expects all people of African descent to fit neatly into one of the media's stereotypes. My father would not have this for me in my own school.

I am a firm believer that children will emulate what they see. Under my father's tutelage, instead of aspiring to be Michael Jordan, I wanted to be Heathcliff Huxtable of *The Cosby Show.* He had a beautiful wife, Claire, who was a lawyer and loving mother, and they lived with their five children in an upscale brownstone in Brooklyn. *The Cosby Show* was the only model of a successful, prosperous, value-centric black family on TV at the time. Instead of hoping to skip college and get drafted onto a professional sports team, I wanted to attend Hillman College from *A Different World*, a spin-off of *The Cosby Show,* which portrayed Denise Huxtable's experience at a fictional HBCU. Even though I grew up watching my fair share of sports and listening to rap (both of which I still enjoy today), I never thought that being an athlete or rap star was one of the few acceptable options for me as a black adult. I had more realistic goals for myself.

As far as my father was concerned, the only option for public school in DC was Benjamin Banneker Academic High School, which Serge attended. Although Banneker had opened its doors as a high school barely a decade prior, it was considered the best public high school in the city. It essentially functioned as a magnet school, pulling in students from multiple districts based on merit. DC is a heavily black city—enrolling students based on achievement meant that Banneker served a large minority population, particularly African Americans. Banneker prided itself on being focused on academics and community service and offered its students advanced-placement classes for college credit. Banneker also had strong ties with Howard University, which was located across the street.

Banneker was not easy to get into. In addition to my high grades and standardized test scores, I also needed to obtain several recommendations, including one from my principal, as well as interview at the school. As a college preparatory school, part of Banneker's educational ethos was to engage its students in rigorous, varied academic experiences; the focus was always on learning and achievement. Extracurricular activities were available, but there was not an abundance of sports—it didn't even have a football team. But that was OK. Every student at Banneker was there for college prep, not for touchdowns and field goals.

Banneker's focus on achievement was evident on its very walls. The sign in its auditorium read "ACHIEVERS" in huge lettering. While the term itself was simple and generic, the banner reminded every single one of us that failure was not an option. The school structured its environment to be inherently supportive: students who performed well were highly praised for their efforts, and those who struggled got the individualized attention they needed. Teachers would engage us on our personal topics of interest, consistently going the extra mile. Administrators carefully balanced outcomes and direction with the pitfall-laden teenage years of their students. Respectful discourse was encouraged, even when—and especially when—students disagreed. We were often reminded of the accomplishments of our school's namesake, Benjamin Banneker. Banneker, the son of a manumitted slave, was the first African American to publish a regular scientific periodical, was heavily involved in designing of the city of DC itself, and even refuted—in a twelve-page letter—Thomas Jefferson's assertion that blacks were inferior to whites, thereby prompting the third US president to publicly reconsider his statement.[11]

My freshman year was the first time I was properly challenged academically. Attending Banneker made me realize that I was no longer the smartest or most gifted student in my class. To earn decent grades, I actually had to work hard. Even the grading scale at Banneker was more rigorous than the national standard. This was a valuable lesson for me that would eventually play a major role in where I am today. I could have coasted through my high school years and earned average grades, but in Banneker's supportive, achievement-centered environment, my drive kicked in. Not putting my best efforts into my studies was no longer an option. I remembered all I'd learned about the struggles of those who fought for my right to an education: their work would not be lost on me. Every quarter, I made it a personal goal to make the dean's list—even if my name was at the very bottom of that list. Always putting my best foot forward was gratifying in itself, but not being at the top of the dean's list gave me something to strive for in the next semester. Thinking back, I can now also appreciate that many of my classmates were brilliant individuals. I may never have been at the very top of the class, but the pond in which I was competing was stocked with highly intelligent and engaged young people, people who are today making lasting impacts on their chosen professions.

Why did so many of my classmates and I go on to achieve success? Was it Banneker's communal, goal-oriented atmosphere? Did the banners proclaiming "GREATNESS IS WITHIN ALL OF US" and similar messages seep into our psyches? Was it the teachers who constantly challenged us? Was it simply self-motivation? Whatever it was, the excellence that resulted was the perfect example of what happens when urban and inner-city black kids are offered an enriching environment and given the opportunity to flourish.

As a part of Banneker's curriculum, students were required to perform a minimum of two hundred hours of community service. Perhaps it was my uncle Paul's influence, but I'd always had an interest in medicine. In ninth grade, I

11 Visit http://www.benjaminbanneker.org/apps/pages/index.jsp?uREC_ID=261778&type=d for a more complete history of Benjamin Banneker Academic High School.

began volunteering at Howard University Hospital (HUH). HUH grew from the Freedmen's Hospital, established in 1862, which was the first hospital in the nation built specifically to treat people of African descent. Many of the Civil War's freed people sought medical help there. Throughout the nineteenth and twentieth centuries, the hospital continued to serve black patients. Its partnership with Howard University created the first historically black teaching hospital. At HUH, I was working with doctors who looked like me, and the patients looked like me as well. Seeing black doctors every day meant that my teenage mind never truly grasped how rare black doctors are. In 2015, only about 5% of practicing doctors in America were black[12]—and I'm sure that percentage was even slimmer during my high school years. Being surrounded by black medical professionals meant I never questioned if medicine was beyond the reach of someone like me.

At HUH, I felt a natural and genuine empathy toward those I was helping to care for. I liked listening as doctors discussed treatments and options, and I found myself wanting to be part of that process so that I, too, could provide the best possible outcomes for those who were ill. I was especially impressed by HUH's outreach programs. Doctors and other staff engaged in health screenings, workshops, and health fairs weekly.

The more time I spent in the hospital, the more I realized that many of the problems facing the individuals in my environment were health-related issues. I noticed that some of the most prevalent diseases in my community were HIV/AIDS, prostate cancer, hypertension, and sickle cell anemia, and I wanted to learn all I could about these conditions. I saw the physicians who treated these patients as people who were an integral part of shaping and strengthening our community. I grew to admire those doctors who served minority populations every day while simultaneously rising to the many challenges associated with a career in medicine. Volunteering at HUH had hooked me: I was going to be a doctor.

---

12 Supporting information can be found at the website of the *New York Times* at http://www.nytimes.com/2015/05/17/opinion/sunday/the-case-for-black-doctors.html.

I knew that becoming a doctor would require more than good grades—it meant that I also had to stay out of trouble. This wasn't as easy as it sounds. While Banneker itself was a safe haven, it was located in one of DC's inner-city neighborhoods. Poverty, crime, and drugs were all prevalent outside the school's walls. Violence was so much a part of the local community that it was extremely difficult to avoid. It wasn't uncommon for me to witness my classmates, and sometimes Howard University students, being harassed, beaten, robbed, and bullied by local gangs or by other kids who went to the surrounding schools. I was never harassed myself, but then again, I was never an easy target. Brownsville had schooled me well in being street.

Why, exactly, were my classmates singled out? Even though we were attending an almost entirely black school, because it was a school you had to test into, many of the neighborhood kids thought we were privileged over them and assumed we thought we were better than they were. Many of the students also surmised that we had more resources than them and thus turned their own anger and frustration outward toward Banneker students. Since many of my counterparts didn't know how to adapt to this environment, they were easy targets for those neighborhood kids who already internalized this falsehood and chafed at the distinction.

I was able to avoid much of the neighborhood's violence until my senior year. At that point in the year, I was beginning to look at colleges seriously and was, for the first time, envisioning a future for myself away from my own home. However, on one particular day, I was walking with my girlfriend and my best friend on my way to the train station. The sidewalk was narrow, with a long chain-link fence bordering us on one side. I spotted a kid approaching us briskly. He was sizing us up and looking for conflict.

I took my girlfriend's hand protectively. She suggested that we cross the street, but I didn't think that was the right move. In Brownsville, I'd learned that showing fear could make you more of a target. Instead, I shot a look to my best friend, alerting him, just as the kid passed by and purposely bumped into my shoulder. This was a deliberate act of aggression. We had made room for him on the narrow sidewalk. I looked him dead in the eye, ready to fight if need be. We exchanged words. Heated, ugly words. But thankfully, nothing more menacing ensued that day.

I thought the incident was over, but roughly two months later, when I was standing alone at a bus stop late one afternoon after an extracurricular activity, a car suddenly pulled up to the curb. The same kid jumped out of the passenger seat. It all happened so fast; I never saw him coming. The next thing I knew, the kid was pushing a gun into my stomach. "Remember me? You ain't so tough with a gun in your face, huh?" he shouted.

My heart fell into my stomach. I had never been so afraid. It was as if I were completely paralyzed, with my jaw wired shut. When I was ordered to run my pockets, I complied. I only had twenty dollars that day, but if I'd been carrying a thousand dollars, I would've parted with it without hesitation. I valued my life and my goals far more than my possessions or ego. Just as importantly, I stayed calm outwardly. I neither showed my fear nor gave this kid a reason to attack further. I was keenly aware that—with just the slightest contraction of his finger on the trigger—this misguided young man could've ended my college dreams, stolen my career in medicine, and put an end to the life I was just beginning to shape for myself.

When the bus came a few minutes later—those few minutes felt like an eternity—all I could think of was how grateful I was to God for sparing my life. My personal survival ethos was always defensive. I tried to look street, but only so I could make it home safely. Walking this line had never been easy. The tension and stress of this balancing act were ever-present undercurrents in my life, but I'd always managed to keep my head above the waves. However, as I boarded the bus that afternoon, I truly felt God had intervened and saved me from a fate that had befallen far too many other urban black men. To this very day, I thank the divine presence that shined on me that afternoon.

As the days passed, I began reflecting on just how different my immediate home environment, especially when I was in Brooklyn, was from the areas in which my homes were located. In the outside world, I learned to be hard and show no fear, as was necessary for urban and inner-city environments. But in my inside world, I was taught responsibility, morals, and respect for others.

Were I not blessed with a safe haven at home, perhaps I would've taken a different path and begun emulating in my teen years the hard mentality of the streets. Perhaps I would've wound up like my attacker, utterly consumed by the survival ethos of the streets and ready to risk injury or even death over a bruised ego.

Now that I'm older, I can appreciate not just what my parents taught me in terms of values but also what they taught me to *expect* from my life. It's only now I understand that by *expecting* me to go to college and have a career and family, they were giving me something to aspire to, to look forward to. By *encouraging* my interests in social issues, and by *supporting* my drive to become a doctor, they gave me possibilities—choices for my own path. But what does the inner-city black male—who perhaps has grown up with nothing but the street model by which to define himself—have to look forward to? For inner-city kids whose lives have been bereft of strong parents, teachers, or other role models, what do they have to strive for?

As my senior year progressed, I increasingly began looking forward to college. I was eager to get out of DC, eager to begin my next phase in life. At this point, I'd been volunteering at HUH for over three years. I was enthusiastic about transitioning from an observer to a student of medicine. I applied to several schools but decided on Xavier University of Louisiana, an HBCU, to which I had earned a partial academic scholarship. My brother, Serge, was already enrolled at Xavier, and I could see how the school was molding him into a well-rounded individual. He had shown me how structured Xavier's curriculum was, and I was especially impressed with Xavier's premed program and its high rates of graduate school placement. I also knew that Xavier took an inclusive and supportive approach toward education, much like Banneker. And so, with all this in mind, after graduating from Banneker, off to New Orleans I went.

CHAPTER 13

The Power of Xavier

MY ACCEPTANCE TO XAVIER UNIVERSITY would not be wasted on me. It was an opportunity that I cherish to this very day. Xavier was founded in 1915 as a high school by Sister Katharine Drexel of the Sisters of the Blessed Sacrament. By 1925, the school had added a four-year college program.[13] From an early age, Sister Katharine had recognized the need to offer educational opportunities to the descendants of America's former slaves. Xavier University is perhaps the crowning achievement of her work, and it remains to this day the only Catholic HBCU in the nation. According to the US Department of Education, Xavier consistently ranks first nationally in the number of African American students earning four-year degrees in the biological, life, and physical sciences.[14]

Stepping onto Xavier's campus for the very first time felt amazingly refreshing. At long last, my late-night study sessions, my acceptance into the National Honor Society, my community service at HUH, my tightrope walk between my home and the streets, and my overall commitment to success had finally paid off. Xavier was my own Hillman College from *A Different World*, and part of me was in awe that I'd been given this opportunity. Here I was, at a nationally ranked university, in an environment of students who not only looked like me but also shared similar career goals and aspirations. I was surrounded by administrators and professors, most of whom were also black, who were dedicated to Xavier's "whole-class" approach to success—that is, instead of competitively

13 Visit the Xavier University website at http://www.xula.edu/about-xavier for more information.

14 Supporting data can be found at the Xavier University website at http://www.xula.edu/about-xavier/index.html.

pitting students against one another and weeding out weaker students, students at Xavier were encouraged to support one another and succeed collectively.

Xavier was the first time I was able to interact with other black students from across the nation. It was the first time I was immersed in an environment dedicated to encouraging black students to express our individual voices, rather than being lumped—as so often happens at even the best-intentioned schools—into one amorphous, catch-all category of "black kids." And of course, Xavier's location in New Orleans exposed me to a city with a unique cultural identity. New Orleans had its own foods, traditions, history, accents, languages, and atmosphere, all of which fascinated and inspired me. My college experience opened my eyes to many things, but first and foremost, it showed me that blackness had many more various expressions than I'd ever dreamed.

I met the man who would become my "second brother" at freshman orientation. Pierre Johnson, one of this book's coauthors, and I immediately struck up a casual friendship. We were both passionate sports fans and hip-hop enthusiasts. Even though we were from different places geographically, the urban environments in which we grew up were eerily similar. I had taken an immediate liking to Pierre, but the bond between us didn't really begin forming until we received the results of our very first biology exam.

I remember the experience vividly, as it was the first in what would become a long line of character-building incidents related to my medical career. My biology exam score was 62 percent, whereas the class average was 77 percent. My self-esteem was crushed. Something had gone terribly wrong. For the very first time, doubt about my academic abilities crept into my mind. I had worked diligently in high school, made the National Honor Society, and earned an academic scholarship to college, yet this test told me I was far, far from the student I believed myself to be. I immediately scolded myself for taking the easy route during my last year of high school. I'd purposely opted out of advanced-placement courses in both biology and chemistry so that I could take less challenging electives instead. A hundred thoughts swirled in my mind. Had I taken a wrong turn somewhere? Had Banneker as a whole left me unprepared for college? Or was I simply not smart enough to pursue medicine?

I couldn't accept grades like this, and despite my doubts, I knew I could do better. I quickly realized that if I wanted to become a physician, I needed far more dedication—and far more hours of studying—to achieve the grade point average needed for acceptance into medical school. The more I thought about that grade of 62 percent, the more I knew the competitor in me was up to the challenge.

I went to the premed office for help. I began attending tutoring sessions, then went to the library after every session for further study. At every tutoring session, I saw the same face. Every night in the library, I again saw the same face: Pierre's. One night, as we were both leaving the library's computer lab, Pierre asked, "Max, do you live here or in the dorms?" My response was, "I actually do live here. I only go to the dorms to shower and brush my teeth!" We both laughed heartily, but as the tone of the conversation turned serious, we realized we were both struggling to adjust to our new environment. Here we were, two young black men, both with lofty dreams of becoming physicians, yet we had both all but failed our first college exam. We talked about our high school achievements and reflected on the feelings of inadequacy and frustration we were both experiencing. It was then that Pierre looked me straight in the eye and declared, "I *refuse* to fail."

The look in Pierre's eye changed everything for me. In that moment, it was almost as if Pierre were a reflection of myself. He had the "eye of the tiger"; it was a toughness and grit I recognized in myself and could well appreciate. I knew then that I had met someone with whom I could fight this battle. I was overjoyed, invigorated, renewed. When Pierre and I began studying together, we made a pact: despite not being the most naturally gifted or talented students, no one would exceed us in drive or dedication. We weren't going to be outworked by anyone. We were two men on a mission, and we were willing to pay the price to get where we needed to be. We knew the price would be sacrificing a lot of extracurricular activities and general college antics, but we didn't care. We did, of course, have some great times in college, but fun was always secondary. We were there at Xavier for one reason. To succeed.

Pierre and I met the third coauthor of this book, Joe Semien, shortly after that night in the library. Like Pierre, I consider Joe a brother as well. Joe was in my physics class, but we'd never really spoken. One afternoon, I could tell that Joe was having a hard time digesting a particular concept. Other schools might have taught me to let Joe flail helplessly, but Xavier's whole-class ethos encouraged us to share our knowledge with our classmates. Many students had done this for me. I helped Joe work through the concept as I understood it. He was truly appreciative. That moment was the beginning of an alliance that has lasted well over a decade.

Joe reminded me a lot of myself—serious-minded, reserved, and full of pride. In Joe, I found the same hunger, passion, and drive that Pierre and I had, and he was as committed to a career as a physician as we were. As our friendship grew, Joe would tell me his stories about growing up in New Orleans and of his subsequent experiences in the US military. These experiences fueled his deep well of mental toughness and dedication.

One of Joe's greatest strengths was his poker face. Whatever the circumstance, he never got rattled, never showed fear. His cool, level-headed demeanor imbued our group with focus, but it also gave Pierre and me even more confidence. We would excel no matter how bleak things seemed in any given moment. The three of us held one another accountable for our actions, ensuring we kept one another motivated and encouraged. With every semester that passed, we never looked too far ahead. Joe taught us that staying in the moment—and rising to it—would bring us to our long-term goals.

The college experience isn't just about studying. No matter how focused a student is, college is a wild and unpredictable time. Pierre, Joe, and I had to balance our studies carefully with the other aspects of student life. Campus life is its own microcosm with its own set of responsibilities. For many of us, it's the first time in our lives when we must decide how we will handle conflict and resolution with our peers in a mature, reasoned way. Of course, all of us can fall short of maturity and reason at times, and there was one instance in particular where our dreams were almost derailed by our own shortcomings.

Pierre's roommate, a close friend of ours, had begun dating a young woman on campus. Unfortunately, her ex-boyfriend, also a student on campus, was not at all fond of this new arrangement. He began exhibiting his jealousy by harassing the new couple. Pierre's roommate reported the harassment to the administration, but since the ex-boyfriend's threats had only been verbal, not physical, security could do nothing to assist.

I remember feeling uneasy every time I heard this story. Something was missing. My gut told me that we didn't have all the facts. I could see how the situation could escalate quickly. If things got out of hand, that would mean potential risk to our friend, to Pierre as his roommate, and to Joe and me as residents of the complex.

Pierre and I decided that we would go speak with the young woman to better assess the situation. When we rang the doorbell, the ex-boyfriend, who was clearly intoxicated, opened the door; his friend—an acquaintance of mine—was beside him. Things turned ugly quickly.

Verbal threats escalated into near violence. As things got more heated, my acquaintance and I questioned what we were about to fight for, and the tense moment resolved itself without the two of us coming to blows. However, when I turned around to address Pierre, I saw him head-to-head with the ex-boyfriend. Oddly enough, Pierre wasn't looking this guy in the eye—he had his head down, as if he were afraid.

"Max, let's roll out," Pierre whispered. I didn't understand: I knew Pierre—it wasn't like him to back down when threatened. In my mind I was screaming, "How can you let this guy think you're afraid of him?" but I kept my mouth shut and followed Pierre outside. Had I missed something in the encounter?

On the way home, I was so frustrated with my brother that I didn't want to talk, but Pierre blurted out, "He's dead!" This made no sense to me. Pierre had just backed off from the conflict. I encouraged him to let it go—we weren't fighting for one of our own girlfriends, after all. I figured the ex-boyfriend regretted his threat. He was a student just like us and was there at Xavier to make a better life for himself. That was when Pierre handed me the missing piece to the puzzle: "Max, he put a knife to my neck!"

I instantly remembered the near paralysis and all-consuming shock from my encounter at the bus stop. I could almost feel that gun against my stomach again. Now I completely understood. Still, I encouraged Pierre to let it go. Perhaps we shouldn't have interfered in the situation in the first place—it really wasn't our battle to fight.

A few days passed, and we thought the situation was over. However, instead of letting bygones be bygones, the ex-boyfriend began bragging on campus that he had "bitched" us and began generally disrespecting us to our peers. After a few days of this, Pierre and I were beyond fed up, and rage and anger consumed us. Being publicly dissed raised the hackles of our street ethos—no one had the right to bad-mouth us. It was the last straw, so to speak, on the pile of ever-mounting stresses and heavy course loads Pierre and I were already struggling against that semester. And this is where both Pierre and I fell victim to the poison that had crept into our hearts: we began plotting revenge.

We found out where the ex-boyfriend lived, and we staked out his apartment—weapons in hand—for hours. Had we found him that night, we would have made the worst decision of our lives. We would've thrown away years of struggle and hard work in one single moment. We weren't just in a dark place that night; we were emulating the behaviors we'd learned in our childhood neighborhoods, reverting back to who we could've become if not for our dedication to improving our lives.

What pulled us to our senses that night was the routine surveillance of the neighborhood police. As a patrol vehicle passed by us in our parked car, I was jolted out of my revenge trance—a jarring so sudden it felt like being startled just before drifting off to sleep. It was as if God Himself had shocked me awake and had opened my eyes to the gravity of what I was about to do—that I was about to throw away my education, sacrifice my future, and possibly take a human life over hurt pride.

I still thank the Lord to this day for offering me clarity that night and for sending the police car. The minute I started plotting revenge, I fell far short of the man I wanted to be. The moment we took steps to implement that plot,

I became nothing but blind fury—a man devoid of reason and maturity and robbed, by my own doing, of my own intellect. Had the Lord not raised me up that night, there's no telling how low I would've fallen. I remain forever grateful.

Even with all the effort we put into our studies, Joe, Pierre, and I were humble enough to know that we needed some guidance and academic tutoring if we were to overcome our next major hurdle, the Medical College Admission Test (MCAT). Here is where the nurturing environment of Xavier's premed program, and the structured and detailed advising it offered, became truly invaluable to us.

Dr. Carmichael was the head of Xavier's premed program, and despite his advancing age, he was an exceptional educator and leader. He knew every student by name, fostered communal learning, and most importantly, always offered all of his students a clear and honest assessment of their progress. Under Dr. Carmichael's direction, premed students formed many independent study groups, where we would share and strengthen one another's knowledge base. I remain friends with many of these students to this day. I'm particularly grateful to Ashte Collins, John Dockins, and Neil Lewis, who all readily shared their innate ability to rapidly teach information that they themselves had just digested. And of course, for Joe, Pierre, and me, these study groups sessions were followed by more trips to the library.

Xavier's premed support program advised that we take the MCAT during the spring semester of our junior year, which we all did. Unfortunately for the three of us, our results were less than stellar. That semester we were all taking especially demanding courses, such as calculus. Frankly, I think our time and effort was stretched too thin to properly prepare for the MCAT. For me personally, standardized tests were never my strength. Yet regardless of the reasons, my brothers and I all had to face our poor MCAT results head-on.

Dr. Carmichael, the premed office staff, and our advisors did not let us give up. During those first three years of college, they had witnessed our determination and effort. They helped us to reformulate our plans. Dr. Carmichael recommended that we finish strongly in our senior year, then move on to Medical/Dental Education Preparatory Program (MEDPREP) courses at Southern Illinois University the following fall. Reps from the program had visited the campus previously, but I hadn't given the program much thought until then. But Dr. Carmichael was right: MEDPREP would allow us to spend a year refortifying the basic science concepts we had learned at Xavier while also giving us the opportunity to work toward improving our MCAT scores. To not be continuing straight on to medical school was disappointing for us all, but if there was a program that could help launch our medical careers, we were going to take full advantage of it.

CHAPTER 14

The Next Level

I GRADUATED FROM XAVIER UNIVERSITY of Louisiana in 2002 with honors and moved on to MEDPREP at Southern Illinois University, Carbondale. MEDPREP's mission is to provide assistance to students in the health-care professions who are educationally or economically disadvantaged, and acceptance is highly competitive. Along with my transcript and recommendation from Dr. Carmichael, my acceptance was dependent on an invitation to, and successful completion of, MEDPREP's Admissions Day, which included approximately six hours of testing, two interviews, and a number of information sessions.

Pierre had also been accepted into the program, but unfortunately, Joe had not, and so his next years would take a different path. Pierre and I spent long hours studying together and building each other up, and I soon flourished under the guidance of mentors such as Dr. Harold Bardo and Dr. Paul Henry. MEDPREP was a well-oiled machine, with all students in the program committed to one another's success. It took a lot of hard work, but I soon found myself at the top of our class.

Although MEDPREP was, in some ways, committed to whole-class success like Xavier, the demographics of Xavier and Southern Illinois University (SIU) were very different. For Pierre and me, SIU was our first experience at a predominantly white collegiate institution. It was clear to us that some of our classmates, and even a few professors—especially those in the greater school, outside of MEDPREP—couldn't grasp the idea of black men succeeding in the medical field. We were even occasionally accused of cheating. Such insulting, unfounded allegations only made us work that much harder.

I vividly remember one incident at the beginning of the academic year when I was struggling to understand a certain concept in one of my courses. I went to my professor's office for assistance. This professor usually taught classes in SIU's medical school and wasn't normally a part of the MEDPREP faculty. After attempting to explain the idea to me, he told me that if I couldn't grasp such a simple concept, I wouldn't do well in his class and probably wouldn't get into medical school. He called my course of study "that MEDPREP program," as if supplementing my undergraduate education were something to be ashamed of—or was perhaps an extra step that only a minority student would need.

I wasn't about to let this professor question my abilities or determination, and he certainly wasn't going to intimidate or dismiss me. Xavier had built up my confidence both as a young man of color and as a student. Instead of reacting emotionally, I calmly but very firmly told him, "Explain it just *one* more time, just so I can make *sure* I understand."

I proved this professor, and all the other naysayers, wrong. By the time the year was over, I had achieved a competitive score on the MCAT, and I was accepted into medical school for admission the following academic year. This thrilled me beyond anything I'd accomplished yet. I was that much closer to becoming a doctor.

My father had always taught me that success wasn't simply about our plans; it was about the *timing* of those plans. Now, as I reflect, I realize just how sage my father's advice truly was: upon graduation, I simply wasn't ready to enter medical school. MEDPREP taught me how to study more effectively; the program offered me instruction on how to digest large volumes of information and retain that information in an accessible, usable way. By spending a year in MEDPREP, I gave myself the opportunity to seize the right timing. Because of this, my years in medical school went about as smoothly as any medical school experience possibly could.

I returned to DC for medical school, enrolling in Howard University's College of Medicine. To this very day, I still remember receiving my acceptance letter from Howard. My joy and elation were overwhelming. My years of hard work, determination, and refusal to accept mediocrity had finally paid off.

Banneker and Xavier had taught me what could be achieved when like-minded individuals come together and form a communal learning environment, and I fully intended to bring this approach with me to medical school. By this point in my life, the whole-class ethos wasn't merely a theory; it had become a cherished value.

My choice of Howard for medical school was based on a number of things—my personal experiences, my worldview, and the factors that I felt had contributed to my previous successes. Just as importantly, Howard stressed preparation for delivering patient care in communities that have a shortage of health professionals, which resonated with me deeply.

What made Howard even more special was that I was going to experience medical school in my home city and at the same hospital where I'd volunteered as a teenager. I would have my family by my side once again. Serge, too, was at Howard. He had enrolled in the School of Dentistry three years earlier. I spent a lot of time with Serge prior to my first semester to get a feel for what professional school was like. Little did he know it back then, but my big brother was always my blueprint, even though we are two very different people. I grew up watching Serge consistently elevate himself, and I was determined to follow in his footsteps. Serge was a generous mentor. He was always willing to give me advice based on his own experiences. Watching Serge, a fourth-year student doing his clerkship, go to his clinic and treat patients became an extra source of motivation for me. Not only was my brother a reminder that my dream was achievable, but because we shared the exact same background, he was an example of my dream being imminently tangible as well.

My first two years of medical school were almost a blur. The feeling of elation from my acceptance letter became a distant memory quite rapidly. I quickly found out that an entire semester's worth of college-level material was often covered in less than a week in medical school. My first two years at Howard were composed of long days in classes and even longer nights of studying. Test after test left little time for any social life. Having my father, who had always been a backbone of support, nearby was an absolute blessing. He would not only uplift me when times were hard but would also play devil's advocate when I felt medical school was unfair or too hard.

Attending Howard also offered another benefit, one that I cannot overstate. Going through my medical school experience with others who looked like myself removed any elements of racial bias I experienced while enrolled in MEDPREP and also offered me a pool of students of African descent whom I could turn to if I needed encouragement or academic help. My personal study group consisted of others to whom I could easily relate. I am especially grateful for the support of Anthony Owusu, a future orthopedic spine surgeon; James Washington, a future neonatologist; Nicholas Henderson, a future physiatrist; and April Wilson, a future family practitioner. Without their support, I never could've navigated medical school's incredibly taxing demands, especially during those first two years.

Looking back, I can understand and appreciate some of the reasons why medical school is so grueling. Patient lives are at stake, and mistakes can exacerbate the problems or, even worse, cost them their lives. This is why all medical students must prove their proficiency by passing the United States Medical Licensing Examination (USMLE) Step 1 before being allowed to continue on to patient treatment in the last two years of school.

Most physicians will tell you that the USMLE Step 1 is the most difficult exam known to humankind. I passed the exam, but despite my long hours of work, I didn't achieve the score I had hoped for. I was afraid that this lukewarm result would later prevent me from being accepted into a residency in my specialty of choice. But once again, I wouldn't let a setback stop me. I'd come too far and worked too hard to give up.

It was during medical school's third year that I truly began to understand what life as a physician would be like. During the third year, medical students rotate through different specialties. My rotations taught me that I was less interested in seeing patients in a clinical setting but that I loved the feeling of being an acute source of care for patients in their most critical moments. Acute care not only requires a strong knowledge base in the sciences but also excellent procedural techniques. An ability to keep both patients and other clinicians calm during periods of heightened anxiety is also essential. For these reasons, I focused on anesthesiology as my specialty.

My clerkship rotations provided me with something greater than I'd ever truly imagined. Having the opportunity to apply the information I had learned during medical school's first two years invigorated me. Through hands-on work with patients, I was finally starting to understand, for example, the intricacies of how the heart, lungs, and other major organ systems worked on a live person. This type of real-world application led to much greater learning retention for me. Thanks to this human component, I also gained the ability to understand how chronic medical conditions could lead to a diverse number of ways patients present to the hospital when they are sick. My ability to visualize complex processes, combined with my ability to act preemptively, quickly caught the attention of my attending physicians. I had chosen my specialty well and received high scores on all my evaluations. By the time the USMLE Step 2 rolled around, I was excited about showcasing my overall improvement and my dedication to my craft.

My USMLE Step 2 results reflected that I had done just that. I scored extremely well. My score, combined with my interviewing skills and letters of recommendation, landed me a residency in anesthesiology—my specialty of choice—at Henry Ford Hospital, a premier Level I Trauma Center.

CHAPTER 15

It's So Cold in the D (Detroit)

THROUGH ALL MY YEARS OF rigorous study, exams, and patient-care experiences, no challenge was greater for me than my first year of residency at Henry Ford Hospital, especially from an emotional standpoint. All the study in the world couldn't ever have prepared me for full-time clinical experience, for treating real people, with all their various illnesses and complications. In my residency, I had to balance all I'd learned in medical school, as well as everything I'd learned on my clinical rotations, with individual patient needs, best possible outcomes, patient preferences and beliefs, and all the complexity of human emotion.

My first residency year in 2008, also known as the intern year, was an emotional rollercoaster of highs and lows. When I think back on that year, I can honestly say that I was depressed. I barely slept, as my patients and their sicknesses kept me up at night. I lost my appetite, which is a common sign of depression, and started losing a lot of weight. I was in such a dark mental state that I sought refuge in isolation and distanced myself from family and friends. If it hadn't been for my beautiful fiancée, Angie, whom I would marry in 2009, praying with me and serving as a source of comfort and strength, I don't know if I would have persevered.

There were many reasons for my depression. Of course, the tribulations of my patients were one contributing element, although I did find joy in successful treatment, especially when the cases were complex. I was also facing an entirely new environment—new city, new job, new associates—that put me completely out of my comfort zone. Huge changes like these would be a challenge for anyone, but I was struggling against something more, too, something that perhaps only other young black professionals can truly relate to.

As a black resident, I knew I was representing not just myself but the whole host of people—those both in my personal life and in the larger historical, cultural sense—who had fought long and hard to make this path possible for me. But I also knew that battling racial bias was far from over. My superiors, peers, and even my patients would carry with them their own prejudices and cultural assumptions. This, in turn, made me feel as though I needed to prove that I belonged, that I needed to work twice as hard to merely be acknowledged as a part of the team.

It's hard to express how greatly being "the other" affected me. On top of all the challenges of my chosen profession, on top of the stress of pushing myself to be the very best physician that I could possibly be, I also had the added weight of feeling personally responsible, on some level, for breaking down stereotypes and divisions. I was extremely hard on myself if I didn't know the answer to an attending's question. I studied case files religiously. I considered every patient assessment and treatment plan in great detail. And I did all of this while also carefully measuring my every word and deed to minimize others' cultural biases. This pressure was overwhelmingly burdensome, draining, ostracizing, and at times, frustrating. I felt as though I were wearing a mask in order to make my peers feel more comfortable with my presence.

Even though I should have sought help, I was afraid to. I worried that if I told my program director, I would be viewed as weak by my superiors. I didn't want to have that stigma attached to me and definitely did not want to potentially delay my residency. I looked at my intern year almost as a rite of passage that I had to endure in order to make it better for the minorities who were to follow in my program. I put it in my mind that I wasn't just doing it for those who had come before me but also for those who were to come after me as well. I felt that if I were to show that I couldn't handle the extra pressures that came with being a minority at my institution, then my superiors would use any negative experience against future residents like me. I should have gone to see a therapist, but in many ways, I played into the stigma that many people do when they are going through a rough patch in life: I refused to acknowledge that something was going on with me, and I was personally ashamed of what others may have thought of me. If I had possessed the strength and courage of my mother, who had already provided a strong blueprint for me on how to tackle mental health issues head-on without losing oneself, I would have gotten better sooner. But going through this helped me understand how important it is to talk about mental health and to share my experiences with others.

I still managed to keep my focus on reaching my dreams and moved through my intern year with guarded caution while struggling to keep myself in a healthy place emotionally. Fortunately, despite the complicated state I found myself in, I did manage to pass the last of my USMLE exams at the end of the year, which made me a fully licensed physician. Once again, I proved to myself that no setback was too great to overcome. My depression began to lift. I knew I could do this.

By God's mercy, that boost came at exactly the right moment because during the first week of my second residency year, which is the year that anesthesia residents start to truly focus on our specialty, I was rudely reminded of how many people view young black men such as myself. While I was in the process of preparing for the first surgery of the day and setting up my workstation, one of the nurse anesthetists barged into my room. She had been on her way to set up her own daily materials but felt the need to interrupt her routine to berate me. She proceeded to tell me that too many supplies were missing from the previous day, then added that I was doing "a poor job of turning over" her cases. "Shape up before we find another tech to replace you," she barked.

I stood there, bewildered, while her rant continued. I would have had every right to verbally fire back, but I didn't say a word—I wasn't about to give in to anger or reinforce her prejudices. When she'd finally talked herself out, I simply grabbed my hospital ID badge from my lab coat and held it up so that she could read the bold lettering: "Madhere, Maxime: MD."

Anesthesia techs are an invaluable part of any surgical team. In a field where seconds count, anesthesiologists' procedures wouldn't go nearly as efficiently without the support of our techs. Yet this nurse had assumed that there was no way I could be one of the new residents. A black man like me had to be a tech.

Although it was true that there were many black techs in our department, neither physicians nor ancillary staff—just like any other role in any other field—are dependent on skin color.

Through her embarrassment, she managed to utter, "I thought you were Mike, our tech." I have to admit, I gained a little satisfaction as her cheeks turned ruddy. Then she managed to make things even worse when she said, "You look just like him. Are you related?" Not only could I not be a doctor in her eyes, but of course, Mike and I *had* to be family—after all, don't all black men look alike, and aren't all black people related?

Even in a majority-black city like Detroit, biases and micro-aggressions like these found their way into my everyday experience. Yet I really did love working in my chosen specialty. Anesthesiology allowed me to apply my procedural and critical thinking skills every day while also letting me follow through with patient care from the surgical procedure itself to recovery. Being knowledgeable about disease processes, then directly implementing hands-on corrective measures to improve patients' quality of life, fascinated and drove me. Because anesthesiology is a specialty that deals with treating patients who meet the criteria for immediate surgical needs, I could see the immediate effects of my actions, which meant that I could continually evaluate my own approach. Additionally, anesthesiology also provided case diversity in the patients I cared for. Managing newborns, adults, pregnant women, and elderly patients—any of whom may have been critically ill with multiple diseases—was a part of a standard workday.

I found my work so energizing and engaging that, by early in my third residency year, I decided to pursue a subspecialty in anesthesiology designated for surgeries involving the heart and lungs, called cardiothoracic anesthesia, and applied for Henry Ford Hospital's fellowship program. The cardiothoracic anesthesiology fellowship would, after I completed all four residency years, extend my time in Detroit by one year, during which I'd be able to focus almost exclusively on my subspecialty training. However, I knew it would be weeks, perhaps months, before I would know if I'd been accepted. All I could do in the meantime was cross my fingers while focusing on my duties as a resident.

The middle of my third year brought glad tidings. My wife told me she was pregnant. We both wanted a fairly large family, and I was elated by the news that our first child was on the way. The timing couldn't have been better, either, as I had just learned that I'd been accepted as a cardiothoracic anesthesiology fellow and would be staying in Detroit for a fifth year. When, a month or two later, we found out that our child was a boy, the sheer bounty and blessings of my life seemed almost unimaginable. We shared the news with our friends and family, and Angie and I even had a name picked out for our little one.

Then, at twenty-three weeks, the unthinkable happened. Angie went into preterm labor. No amount of medical intervention could stop her contractions, and our tiny son came into this world much, much too early. I vividly remember holding our baby in my arms as we watched him take both his first and last breath of life. I never knew until that moment just how deeply the human heart could break.

We cried and grieved for months. What was supposed to be one of the happiest moments of our lives threw me into a profound, indescribable darkness. However, I knew that I had to be strong for my wife, just as she had been strong for me during my intern year. Plus, I still had to complete my residency, even though every day was a struggle. If there was any fortune in my life at that moment, it was the discipline of all my previous years of training. I called on that strength and managed to complete my third residency year.

By the grace of God, Angie conceived again in the fall of my fourth residency year. After losing our son, we were torn between ecstasy and fear, but we trusted in God and prayed for a healthy pregnancy. Those nine months were some of the most stressful of our lives. Our joy and excitement were perpetually tempered by anxiety and fear. Angie was in and out of the hospital throughout the pregnancy. Sometimes her visits were for preventative procedures and prenatal care, but we did face a number of emergency situations as well. But no matter the cost, we were committed to bringing our daughter into the world in the healthiest state possible.

Our faith and commitment were rewarded—but not before we faced an eleventh-hour, extremely agonizing challenge. Angie's pregnancy reached a full term of thirty-eight weeks, but during labor, she experienced a serious complication called placental abruption. This is when is the placenta detaches from the uterine wall. Placental abruption is a fairly rare condition, and in most cases, it happens well before the onset of natural labor. The condition is usually manageable by precautionary, third-trimester care, but when a placental abruption occurs during labor, the situation is extremely dangerous to both mother and child. Angie was bleeding so heavily, and our sweet daughter was in such distress, that the doctors had to perform an emergency cesarean to save both their lives.

Gabrielle, our beautiful gift and perfect miracle, came into the world almost exactly one year after we had lost her brother. In this sense, her arrival was tinged with a bittersweetness, but the sweet far outweighed the bitter. When I held my baby girl for the first time, I knew nothing would ever be more important than my role as her father. I vowed to be a strong, loving father to Gabby—and to all my children to come—just as my father had always been to me.

The whirlwind of Angie's pregnancy, the complications of Gabrielle's birth, and the longer-term postpartum care that Angie needed did put a great deal of stress on me in terms of successful completion of my residency. By the time Gabrielle arrived, my board exam was only a few weeks away. I knew I was underprepared, but my family had to, and always would, come first. Studying and supplemental research took a back seat by necessity. I did all that I could to prepare for the board exam in the remaining few weeks, but ultimately, I was not successful. Not passing was disappointing but not surprising. I am a father and a husband even before I am a doctor. Yet my poor exam result did nothing to deter me. I retook the board exam at the earliest possible date and passed with flying colors.

As a board-certified anesthesiologist, I was then able to move on to my cardiothoracic anesthesiology fellowship. My fellowship was an amazing experience. In pursuing such an elite subspecialty, I finally felt myself transforming into the physician I always knew I could be. As my fellowship year progressed, I was able to use and refine my unique skills daily to help improve the lives of critically ill patients. I found joy in my craft, and I do believe that my love for my work translated into more positive patient outcomes.

Because cardiothoracic anesthesia is a highly specialized area of medicine, at the end of my fellowship, I needed to pass one last board exam to earn my diplomate in advanced perioperative transesophageal echocardiography. With this certification, I became one of the nation's most highly accredited anesthesiologists.

I had begun looking for permanent positions outside of Detroit as the end of my fellowship approached. After graduating from my fellowship in 2013, I interviewed at a number of hospitals, but when I was presented with a staff physician offer at a medical center in Baton Rouge, I knew it was the right choice for my family and me. I'd visited Baton Rouge, which is just over an hour away from New Orleans, a few times while I was at Xavier, and Angie had grown up in the area. We could put down roots here, watch our family grow and thrive here. Although I'd never spent money frivolously, soon after moving, I gave myself a graduation gift: a BMW 7 Series, a car that I'd dreamed of for years. In every sense, Baton Rouge felt like home.

As I walked into my new hospital on my first day of work, some great mixture of accomplishment, pride, relief, joy, and awe washed over me. I remembered my grand-mère's words. I had fulfilled my duty and brought "progress" to the family. After a decade of dedication and struggle, after a lifetime of mainstream society telling me that I couldn't, I had finally reached my goal. As the black son of immigrant parents, and as a child of the streets, my path could have taken many, many other routes. Yet with self-determination, the support of my family, and the dual blessings of Xavier and Howard Universities, I learned that no achievement was out of reach, that I was not excluded from any dream, no matter how big. For my dream was not a dream deferred. It was a dream pursued, fought for, supported, and ultimately, realized.

CHAPTER 16

Physician, Father, Black Man, and Citizen

As of this writing, it has been nine years since my intern year, and much has changed in both my personal and professional life. Angie and I were blessed with our second daughter, Vivienne, in 2015, and our son, Kingston, arrived in 2016. I have the home I always dreamed of, the family I always wanted, and the career I worked so tirelessly to attain. These accomplishments give me a great sense of satisfaction in knowing that I have achieved many of the goals I'd set for myself, and I couldn't be more grateful for these many benisons. Yet there is still a hunger inside, a yearning for more. As a physician, I make significant decisions every day that affect the lives and outcomes of my patients, but I've come to realize that the decisions I make in the nonprofessional parts of my life aren't that much different. My dedication to becoming a better husband, father, friend, and role model motivates me every day.

I still wake up every morning asking God for further clarity on my path in this life. As I hear all the voices in my mind vying for attention, three questions always seem to shout the loudest: Am I doing enough? Can I do more? How far-reaching are my obligations to those who will follow me?

In my adopted home city of Baton Rouge, African American men have a 46 percent high school graduation rate, and one-third of African Americans live below the poverty line.[15] In Haiti, the country from which I draw my heritage,

15 Supporting information can be found at the Schott Foundation for Education website at http://urban-congress.artimization.net/wp-content/uploads/Study.pdf. These data reflect 2011–12 statistics.

59 percent of the population lives on less than two dollars per day, 50 percent of children do not attend school, and the overall literacy rate is roughly 60 percent.[16] Every day, I ask myself what I can do to help improve the lives of the individuals who are reflected in these disturbing statistics. I do what I can, however I can. I mentor teenage boys who lack strong male role models through my work with 100 Black Men of Metro Baton Rouge. I am a member of the Urban Congress on African American Males in Baton Rouge, an advocacy and activist group that seeks to identify and expand the strengths of black males and local black communities. I am a role model to my children, who will someday pass our family's values and strength on to their own children. Yet nothing ever seems quite enough. I want to do—and I will do—more.

On a more intimate level, I know I am a part of a demographic that suffers from the preconceived notions that keep this country divided. This is apparent in every aspect of my life, not just because I'm one of the 5 percent of this country's practicing black doctors. This is why I can be driving home in the "fancy" car that I worked over a decade to earn, get stopped by law enforcement for the "crime" of driving six miles per hour over the speed limit, be suspected of possessing drugs or weapons, and have my entire person and vehicle searched. If I am not docile or meek enough in my tone of voice or body language, I risk being perceived as aggressive or confrontational. One wrong move could mean my life. This is also why I can walk into a patient's room and initially be mistaken for a member of the maintenance staff, assumed to be there to clean the room. Without any exaggeration, both of these examples—and many more not recounted here—have been a part of my existence since I earned my board certification. No matter my accomplishments or my training, I will always be subject to the assumptions society at large is trained to make about black men.

To be quite honest, believing that racial inequity will ever improve can sometimes be quite difficult. Nonetheless, I strive to remain positive and sustain my drive. I find inspiration and hope in both the great and the small. Having gone through the process of writing this book with my brothers, I am hopeful that our stories might speak to a young reader and offer him or her some degree

16 Supporting data can be found at the World Bank website at http://www.worldbank.org/en/country/haiti/overview and at the Haiti Partners website at https://haitipartners.org/about-us/haiti-statistics.

of support or direction; who knows what sharing our stories might lead to? Perhaps someday, one of our readers will go on to change the world.

I carry with me a famous quote by African American author and social critic James Baldwin: "Not everything that is faced can be changed, but nothing can be changed until it is faced." I try to face racial challenges by doing my small part in reversing the tide—by volunteering and mentoring youth, by being a positive role model, and by ensuring that my children have all the resources needed to achieve their own successes. Holding myself to this standard is not easy, but I do find myself modestly encouraged when I encounter other young black professionals. Although our personal stories are certainly different, I know we all share a common sense of faith, a belief that we ourselves can be Baldwin's change.

BOOK III

Joseph's Story

Foreword

"God grant me the serenity to accept the things I cannot change; courage to change the things I can; and wisdom to know the difference."

—The Serenity Prayer

Some individuals are blessed to face few life-changing obstacles. Their purpose in life is easily defined, but others find themselves on more turbulent paths. In my own life, it took a while before I could open my heart and allow God to reveal His purpose for me, but when He finally did, He sent me on a journey that has ultimately brought me happiness, personal fulfillment, and the privilege of caring for both my family and my patients.

From a young age, my mother always taught me that I would face many trials and tribulations. She was right. My path has been a long one, but it has always been filled with God's mercy and grace. We can always feel a sense of security, even when we make mistakes—I know this to be true from my own experiences. Among so many wonderful gifts, we are given the blessings of determination and vision. To this day, I am still learning what is in store for me as I continue to pray for guidance.

On these pages, I will share some of my deepest, darkest secrets and insecurities. By writing this book, I am releasing my own sense of pride. I've often tried to erase these secrets from my memory, but denying my past would be untrue to myself. Every time I revisit my dark places, I become more grateful for my past experiences because each and every piece of my existence has brought me to my life as it is now. By every statistic, I should not be where I am today, but with God's mercy, I have accomplished all that I set out to do, and I have received joys in my life that I never even thought were possible.

I pray that my two sons, Joseph III and Miguel, will one day read this and understand the many trials and tribulations I've faced, and I hope they will know that my early mornings, long nights, and occasional extended absences were all for them. I have been driven in my work and on my life's path so that someday my sons will be able to reach their own potentials. My wife and I strive to give our boys every tool and resource possible to achieve success, no matter the sacrifice. I want my children to learn from my past so that they don't repeat my missteps and so that they don't fall into the dark places I once visited. My desire is for my children to dream bigger than I have dreamed, to reach heights far higher than I have.

To the world: I hope my story reaches a young person in need of a real-life example of what can be accomplished through determination, hard work, and sacrifice. There are no odds so great that they can't be overcome. I share my story with the hope that it will be a small encouragement that will help young men and women push forward and fulfill their dreams.

CHAPTER 17

The Premise of Principles

My father is a man of few words, but he has always had an incredible work ethic, and when he does speak, every word is deliberate and commands attention. The first job I can remember my father having was at a janitorial services company, where he was a crew leader. His wages barely kept us above poverty, and providing for a family of six was not always easy. But he is a good, honorable man who raised us well; everything he earned went toward the family, although it was my mother who managed the household accounts. Even when the light bill wasn't paid, and we had to make do without electricity, we always had food on the table, and we were fortunate in that my parents owned our home outright due largely to a lawsuit my mother had won. Even though my mother could stretch a dollar further than anyone else, our budget was very tight until well into my teen years. I remember my parents always fussing about money, but my childhood years were some of the happiest years of my life.

When I was ten years old, my mother took me aside and told me that my father couldn't read. This surprised me, especially because my father often drove us to places we had never been before without any need for a map. My mother then explained that words over three letters were impossible for my father to read. He was functionally illiterate. I remember him repeating the word *red* on a few occasions; "R-E-D, R-E-D," he would mumble to himself. But my father has always been very intuitive, and he hid his inability to read well. He has made his way through life remarkably, despite this disadvantage. Today, I am more than thankful for the determination he instilled in me, for in my earlier years, I could not see just how great this gift was.

By the time I was a teenager, my father had taken a job at Avondale Shipyard on the bank of the Mississippi River, which was about twenty miles upriver from New Orleans. Here he had the honor of building ships for the US Navy. My father's incredible work ethic caught the attention of his superiors. He was offered a foreman's position that entailed supervising hundreds of other employees and came with a substantial pay raise. Yet my father knew this job would require scouring reports, maintaining contracts, and writing numerous documents. His honesty would not allow him to take the position in good conscience. Instead, he was completely frank and told his supervisor about his illiteracy. The supervisor then told my father to never repeat his secret to anyone, then gave my father the job anyway. Admitting his trouble with reading was truly a humbling experience for my father, but coming clean gave him an overwhelming confidence. He learned that there were no limits to his success regardless of his shortcomings. This was the first time I can recall witnessing such true resilience in the face of obstacles. My father's bravery and determination enabled him to fulfill his own destiny.

My parents have always had a special bond—they've been together for over forty years. They are true partners and helpmates to each other. In my teen years, my mother helped fill the gap of my father's illiteracy from behind the scenes. She assisted him with his paperwork, read reports to him, and quietly helped with his administrative work. She did of all this while caring for my sisters and me, working in our church, and struggling with illness. My mother was born with a condition called Arnold Chiari malformation, which is a defect in the brain that puts extra pressure on the cerebellum. Because the cerebellum is the part of the brain that controls balance and fine motor skills, my mother later developed balance issues and sometimes experienced spells of dizziness and even paralysis. These symptoms were accompanied by extreme fatigue and headaches.

As a young boy, I remember being terrified that my mother would die, and I know my sisters felt this too. I remember praying daily, asking God to heal her. I am thankful that my mother's dying never came to pass—she's alive and well to this day—but the fear of losing her cast a heaviness over my young life. Any time she had an attack, the terror in me was renewed, time after time, year after year.

My mother's relationship with God has always been a defining aspect of her life, and she wanted the same for each of her children. She always said, "Prayer should be your daily connection with God." We would pray in church, at home, and in the car, plus it was our custom to pray together every time we left the house. We attended Bible studies, Sunday school, Sunday morning services, and Sunday evening services, and my sisters all sang in the church choir. My mother taught us that God is our protector, healer, and close friend. She created a foundation through which God's light could enter our lives. Certainly, I strayed from His light at times, but God is all-forgiving: He welcomed me home no matter my transgressions.

I am the third child in my family and my parents' only son. My oldest sister was a handful. She was sometimes mischievous and often found herself in trouble, but she had a loving heart and cared for those around her deeply. She didn't always earn the best of grades in school, but she was determined to achieve her goals and was the first of my siblings to attend college. My second-oldest sister was the "angel" of the family. She was respectful, kind, and smart, and her teachers at school and at church were delighted in having her as a student. She was also quite a tomboy. She could run faster, climb a tree quicker, and throw a football farther than anyone I knew. My baby sister was a sweet and innocent girl, and my bond with her has always been particularly strong. As my only younger sibling, she always looked to me for protection and guidance.

My mother constantly told me that it was my responsibility to look after all my sisters, even though I was a middle child. I took this to heart. Even when I began to stray from family life, I always tried to take care of my sisters. Today, I am proud to say that each of my sisters is a college graduate and has a career of her own.

As a child, I had over fifty cousins, and that number later increased drastically during my adult years. Both my parents' families were large. My father had eleven siblings, and my mother had seven. All of my aunts and uncles had families of their own, leading to scores of cousins for me to play with. Despite our size, my extended family was close. My grandparents, who lived about two hours outside of New Orleans, had a country farm. Summers with them gave my cousins and me all kinds of opportunities to use our imaginations. My grandparents' farm had chickens, pigs, cows, horses, and all manner of animals to play with, and I spent many afternoons exploring the acres of woods behind their farm. Even in my neighborhood, we relied on our imaginations to dream up our own fun. We would build bridges, dig trenches, and create entire construction sites for our Tonka trucks. One particularly fine creation consisted of a mansion with a moat around it. We filled the moat with water and caught a lizard to be the "alligator" that protected our property. I loved living so close to the banks of the Mississippi—there were all sorts of wetland animals for me to chase after and play with.

I've always had a passion for living things. I love the idea of life—be it human, animal, or insect—and as a child, I studied the farm animals with curiosity and wonder. Maybe I had an early inkling of becoming a doctor, or perhaps a vet, but I kept this idea to myself. I had never met a doctor except for my pediatrician. Everyone I knew was working-class, like us; being a doctor simply wasn't a part of my world.

"It takes a village" is probably the best way of describing the neighborhood of my early youth. In our working-class neighborhood, all parents had a hand in watching over all kids. If another parent saw me acting out, my mother was sure to get a phone call. My mother had even given permission to a few specific parents to slap my hand when it was warranted. We attended a small, close-knit family church of about one hundred members. Our church was a family—in both the figurative and literal sense. It seemed like everyone in the church was related in one way or another. I think we were one of the few families that wasn't related to the pastor himself. However, the pastor was related to one of our neighbors, and we all took vacations together as if we were family. Our church hosted picnics and other events, including family reunions. My mother had a hand in most of these events and made sure that all four of her children did too. All the kids in the church loved having Bible quiz challenges with nearby churches: we would recite verse after memorized verse from the King James Bible, and we felt no small amount of pride when winning championships.

My neighborhood in Jefferson Parish probably wasn't idyllic as I remember, but to me, it was a safe and secure corner of the world. Things began to change drastically, though, when I was six or seven years old. Unfamiliar families started moving in, and instead of having clean fun and roughhousing, real arguments began cropping up, and tempers often flared. Fights became commonplace. My mother became concerned for our safety.

My mother decided it was time for me to learn how to defend myself and protect my sisters. I knew my father was slow to anger but was also able to defend himself physically when pushed. His long working hours kept him away from home, so my mother stepped in and gave me some lessons in self-defense. She taught me different defensive techniques but always emphasized the importance of never hitting a woman. Every so often, I would have to defend myself or my sisters, and I was proud to tell people that my skills came from my mother.

My neighborhood would get rougher and rougher in the coming years. I changed along with my environment. This change wasn't always for the better.

Starting kindergarten made me very nervous, but I was comforted to have my two best friends with me. We weren't in the same class, but we sat together at lunch and played together at recess. I don't remember a lot about kindergarten, but I clearly remember how proud my parents were when I finished the year. At my "graduation" ceremony, my parents were so proud that I might as well have been a child prodigy who was graduating with my doctorate. I wanted to put that look of pride on my parents' faces again and again.

Many young children have speech issues that resolve on their own, but by second grade, it was clear that I had a speech impediment: I stuttered badly. My school initially thought I had a hearing problem and tested me, but my ears were fine. Occasionally, I was too embarrassed to speak in class, and I can recall a few incidents where I got into fights when the other kids teased me for my stutter. My mother worked very hard to help me pronounce words that were difficult for me. It took a good number of years before I could get my words out easily. I credit my mother for her patience and persistence.

Third grade was a pivotal moment for me. I started to become more concerned with my image in school and began having trouble with impulse control, which became a defining aspect of the rest of my youth. Some part of me was angry, although to this day, I can't say exactly why. All I know is that I hated being embarrassed, and when I was embarrassed, I lashed out. This was particularly true with authority figures. My young mind was confused. On the one hand, I'd been taught to defend myself and have my say, but on the other, I was taught to respect my elders. It was difficult for me to determine which teaching applied to which situation, and that only made me angrier.

The first time I lashed out was one afternoon when my teacher began lecturing me about my behavior. My desk was at the front of the class. Everyone could see her criticizing me, and I turned around to see my classmates' reactions. This frustrated my teacher, so she pushed my legs back under my desk. Without thinking, I stood up and hit her.

I instantly knew what I had done was wrong, yet I felt justified in defending myself. My teacher, clearly shocked, sent me straight to the principal's office. I tried to defend my actions when my mother arrived, but she was furious with me and mortified by my behavior. The principal ordered that I be suspended for several days, but his punishment didn't satisfy my mother one bit. She marched me back to my classroom and made me apologize to the teacher in front of everyone. Then she truly humiliated me by taking out a belt and whipping me in front of the whole class. I remember staring my classmates in their eyes, daring them to laugh. I told them with my expression that if I saw the smallest smile, I would retaliate. I thought I would see mocking in my classmates' eyes, but instead, I only saw shock. Eventually, I began to cry silently, not because of the whipping but because my heart hurt. My mother was teaching me humility. It was a painful lesson.

When I returned to school after my suspension, I was ashamed of the way I'd treated my teacher, but I was also nervous because I was worried about my reputation. This was my first real experience with inner struggle. One minute I wanted be a good student and make my mother proud, but the next minute, I felt I needed to prove to my classmates that I wasn't weak. This was a confusing mix of emotions for a young boy.

Ultimately, this incident taught me about forgiveness, love, and self-sacrifice. Once back in class, I learned that my teacher had enjoyed having my sister as a student the previous year and had been looking forward to my being in her class. But then I had struck her. She must have felt angry and embarrassed, possibly even betrayed. Yet my teacher, demonstrating amazing self-sacrifice and love, forgave me. In fact, she had been the greatest advocate for the principal's lifting my suspension. I wanted to make things right with her. For the rest of the year, if anyone dared say something negative about her, I was her champion and defender. I never disrupted her class again, and I became her best student. By her example, my teacher taught me how to see the potential in others and how to truly love and care for those who've made mistakes.

Like many eight-year-old children, I had trouble applying the lessons I'd learned intellectually to my emotions and actions. I managed to behave in class and earned good grades, but later that year, I landed myself in trouble again. My friends and I had just learned to make spitballs, and the novelty made them great fun. One afternoon, the driver of our school bus caught me launching a big, wet spitball. He ordered me to the front of the bus and demanded my teacher's name.

I truly couldn't pronounce my teacher's name because of my speech impediment, but I didn't want my friends to know this. Instead, I pretended that I didn't know her name. This infuriated the bus driver, who threatened to drive me back to school and leave me there. When we arrived at my house, he let my sisters off the bus but refused to let me exit. When the doors slammed shut, panic welled up in my chest. I felt caged, like an animal. My heart began racing, and I screamed for my sisters to get my mother. I felt utterly imprisoned and began kicking and punching anything between the doors and me—and the bus driver took a direct hit to the eye. His glasses flew off, and he threw me to the floor. I could clearly see him struggling to keep control of himself. Fortunately, he let me off the bus and quickly drove away rather than letting his anger get the best of him.

The next day, I was suspended from school again, this time for an entire week. Confusion and frustration plagued my young mind. I had felt threatened by the driver and had defended myself, yet at the same time, I knew, once again, that what I had done was wrong. My oldest sister called me a disgrace and reminded me that I had been raised to behave better. I pretended her words didn't bother me, but I was secretly distraught and ashamed. I knew I was embarrassing the family. I also realized that I hadn't considered how my actions would affect others—my sisters still had to ride that bus every day, after all.

Not long after this incident, a kid from my neighborhood started an argument with me, which turned into an all-out fistfight. I found myself in the principal's office again. The principal called my mother and told her that I needed to be placed in special education classes due to my repeatedly disruptive behavior. I was shocked. I was an honor-roll student—I didn't need special education. My mother was furious, too, because she knew I wouldn't be challenged academically in special education classes. She flat out refused to let the principal move me to a new class. I was grateful and proud that my mother had my back, yet I knew that I needed to control my emotions and learn to make better decisions. Unfortunately, I had no idea how to do that. Every time I lashed out, I felt worse and worse, which only fueled the anger and frustration inside of me.

Fourth and fifth grades were marked by similar incidents. I always made good grades, but I was also always in trouble. I sometimes thought about becoming a doctor, but I never really talked about it. Some of my aunts and uncles already treated me as if I wouldn't amount to much, and it was all too easy for me to internalize their attitudes. And anyway, medicine didn't seem realistic for a kid like me who was always in the principal's office.

Organized sports, basketball and football in particular, provided some outlet for my aggression, and I began hanging out with the kids whose families had recently moved into our neighborhood. None of these kids was a part of our church family, and for the first time, I was no longer under the constant eye of my mother and her friends.

As my friends and I prepared for middle school, we admitted quietly to one another that it was scary to think about. We knew the kids in sixth grade would be bigger and the classes would be larger. We were already feeling overwhelmed. I was now on the precipice of puberty, and my image had become all the more important to me. On the first day of school, I made sure to wear the trendiest clothes and the finest shoes, determined not to give the older kids any reason to mock me.

In sixth grade, we started learning about anatomy. I was intrigued by the many bones, tendons, organs, cavities, and tissues of the human body, and I was even more enthralled by how all these elements combined to make a living, breathing human being. I think this was my first real interest, scientifically speaking, in medicine. The idea of operating on the human body excited me. It was all so fascinating. Yet at the same time, I was afraid of being called a geek or nerd if I showed too much interest. I had always kept up my grades, so thankfully, earning good marks in science didn't raise any eyebrows among my friends, but I was still hungry to learn more. Having to hide my interest only added fuel to my anger. The human body was such an amazing mystery, yet peer pressure told me I couldn't explore my passions.

It was around this time that my grandmother came to stay with us for a while. She had diabetes and was on insulin. One afternoon, my curiosity spurred me to take her spent needle out of the garbage so that I could inject a lizard with rubbing alcohol and "operate" on it. I didn't want to harm the lizard, only learn from it. After opening its abdomen, I sutured the lizard back up to see if it would move again. It didn't. My first "surgery" was a resounding failure, but that didn't deter my interest. I didn't tell anyone about this, though. My friends would have teased me, and my parents surely would've punished me.

By the eighth grade, I had two different groups of friends: my childhood friends with sound family values and deeply involved parents and my new friends, who had less parental supervision and fewer rules. I thought my new friends were a lot cooler than my old friends. I was drawn to their freedom and independence, and I started hanging out with them more and more. Beyond the sight of my mother's watchful eye, I began handling myself my own way. For me, that meant I would start swinging if the slightest thing didn't go my way. Anytime I was challenged or embarrassed, I fixed it with my fists.

CHAPTER 18

Darkness and Light

IN NINTH GRADE, I EARNED the nickname of "Lil' Joe" along with the reputation of being a fighter. I liked this image and assigned myself as the protector of my older sisters while at school. My high school was one of the largest in Louisiana, with almost three thousand students. The student body was very diverse ethnically, but most students came from modest neighborhoods like mine. As in most high schools, students formed cliques quickly. My clique wasn't the most popular, but we were respected because we could hold our own when we needed to.

In tenth grade, my clique and I began wearing white T-shirts to identify ourselves. We weren't an official gang, but we definitely had a group identity, which was partly rooted in protecting our neighborhood. One afternoon, my older sister came to me crying because someone had assaulted her. There was no way I could let this stand. Without hesitating, my friends and I took the matter into our own hands and beat the guy responsible very badly. I remember feeling a sense of sadness. I could have stood up for my sister without the violence. I only beat this kid to protect my reputation.

I was suspended for a considerable period afterward. When I came back to school, I was told that if I were absent for even one more day, I would have to repeat the entire year. I worked very hard to finish the year without missing any more school, and I achieved grades with honors. It wasn't always easy to maintain my grades without looking "too smart," but I managed it somehow.

By tenth grade, our neighborhood had changed considerably. Drugs were common, and incidents of violence were on the rise. During my sophomore year, a new family moved into the neighborhood, and I became friends with a massive, 240-pound football player. He was nearly six and a half feet tall and towered over all of us. My friends and I knew he was selling drugs and involved in other criminal activities, but he watched over us at school and warned us to stay away from that kind of life. I wish I had listened.

It was also in tenth grade that my mother's Chiari malformation began affecting her far more severely. She started experiencing episodes of temporary paralysis. She had a bell she would ring when she felt the onset of an episode, and my sisters and I would run to her bed. We'd immediately prop her up, which helped her to regain function. Sometimes at night, I would hear the bell and rush to help my mother, only to find that the ringing was in my head. This was the most terrifying period my fourteen-year-old-self had ever faced. Yet regardless of the emotional and mental exhaustion my sisters and I experienced from caring for our mother, this was one of the first times that love, however tempered with fear, played a transformational role in my life. I was determined to be a factor in my mother's survival.

The doctors told my mother she needed surgery on her brain to stop the attacks. This struck fear in the heart of our entire family, especially because the surgery had to be done right away before any further damage was done. I was now old enough to understand the risks that came with surgery, and I spent countless nights praying for her protection. Prayer was always our practice, but this was the first time I prayed with an adult mind-set about such a grave issue. I began to see God for His greatness and healing. He offered me a love and comfort I'd never consciously felt before. Even still, on the day of the surgery, I hugged my momma tight, fearing I might never see her again.

Fortunately, the procedure went well. But my mother's recovery took about two months and was very hard on her. She cried a lot from the pain. My father still worked long hours, so I took it upon myself to take care of my sisters and take on as much responsibility as I could because I wanted my mother to focus on healing. I already felt that I was the protector of my sisters like my mother had taught me to be, but now I tried to be their parent too. This was a lot of stress for a teenage boy. I couldn't show that stress at home, so I let it out on the streets.

By the time I was in eleventh grade, our neighborhood had become overrun with drugs, and with drugs came elevated levels of violence and crime—fights and shootings had become all too common. Both ends of my neighborhood were now riddled with drugs, and my family was living right in the middle. My friends and I started associating with older kids who were dealing drugs. I was no longer the church kid my mother had raised me to be, and I began selling drugs, out of my own curiosity and eagerness to be independent.

Before I could fully process what I was doing or how quickly my life had changed, running from the police and dodging gunfire became regular occurrences for me. A good number of my friends were arrested and sent to prison. Far, far too many more wound up in the morgue. I was constantly afraid of being either robbed or killed, but I never dared show weakness or fear. Soon came the moment when my clique had a beef with another group. My friends and I armed ourselves and waited anxiously for their car to pass through our neighborhood. This was a moment of clarity for me—I now truly understood that I was heading down a dark path. The very hands I secretly hoped to use for healing were ready to do harm instead.

I was living a double life. I would attend church on Sunday mornings but would be out selling drugs by Sunday night. I was soon making more money than I'd ever seen in my entire life. I didn't want my parents to know what I was doing, of course, so I was careful to never take the drug money home. To avoid suspicion, I saved almost all the drug money I earned and mowed lawns to make it appear as if my pocket money came from honest work. My parents didn't know it, but I begin to put aside all my childhood endeavors, such as playing high school football. Selling drugs took up most of my time and was far more lucrative financially.

My parents expected me to go to college, like my older sisters. Because I was hiding so much and maintained high grades, my parents still believed that I was a good kid and still thought I could get into a decent school. I knew, however, that the path I was heading down would lead me to jail or death. Because I had a reputation as a thug, my teachers and school administrators didn't expect much from me. All this only reinforced those aunts and uncles who didn't expect me to achieve, and it was easy for me to believe that my worst self was my true self. Plus, very few of my friends were thinking about college. None of our parents had professional-level careers, and none had gone to college. Higher education wasn't an expectation for most of us. However, my parents knew the value of an education and insisted that I speak with my guidance counselor about available college opportunities. I took their advice, but when I spoke with my counselor, she flatly suggested that a trade might be a better option for me, even though I was a solid B student. Despite my grades, she believed I was not college material because of my behavior.

In my senior year, a good friend of mine was applying to colleges. He pushed me to apply too. I was sick and tired of the low expectations everyone had for me, and I turned that anger into my impetus. I still had a passion for living things, still thought deep down that I could be a doctor—perhaps even a neurosurgeon. But it was now undeniable that my street life could have a real impact on my future, even if I managed to stay out of jail. With the hope of turning my life around, I followed my friend's lead and applied to a number of colleges. Even though so much of my life was tangled up in drugs, I also began distancing myself from selling drugs as much as I could. This wasn't easy because I didn't know how to get out of the street life I'd created for myself. A part of me felt trapped.

By my senior year, I had earned enough credits that I was able to enroll in a program that allowed me to work the later part of the day. I got a job at a bank, where I worked with an elderly white gentleman. Despite my background, this man saw potential in me, and my confidence grew as he began mentoring me. He had a huge impact on my view of myself and the world at large. He taught me the importance of honest work, good credit, and smart investments. I still apply the principles he taught me to this day, and I will always appreciate the patience, kindness, and time he offered me. The simple act of this man's faith in me made a huge difference in my attitude. When I graduated high school only a few months later, I felt better about myself than I had in a very long time.

While I was working at the bank, I had been accepted into Xavier University of Louisiana and had declared my premed major right away. When I started taking my first biology courses, I was reinvigorated. However, I quickly found out that the environment and academics at Xavier were very different from high school. I was unprepared both academically and socially, and I struggled with adjusting to college life. The classes were huge, overwhelming, and much more intense than anything I'd experienced in high school. Although I worked hard, my first-semester grades were disappointing. I began to think the doubts of my aunts, uncles, and high school teachers were well founded.

Because Xavier was only a few miles away from home, I never divorced myself completely from my illegal activities. My neighborhood and reputation still hung over my head, and the street life was weighing me down, even as I was fighting to pull myself back up. This created a great strain. I felt trapped once again, caged in from every angle.

I decided I needed a drastic change to free myself. At the end of my first semester, I decided to join the military with the intention of becoming a medical specialist. This felt like my chance to start over fresh and put the past behind me. As a medical specialist in the US Army, I would still have a career in medicine while also serving my country. On the day that I enlisted, I remember being overly excited. My life would change dramatically, and I'd be free of the violence and street life that still plagued me.

I knew the military would transform me into a better man. In all honesty, the 1994 movie *Forrest Gump*, which chronicled the life of a disabled but deeply good-hearted man, inspired me to sign up. The film had shown me how transformative army life could be. I was sure the army would correct any deficiencies I had while molding my life for the better. The army meant I'd be away from New Orleans, away from my reputation. I could become anyone I wanted to be.

I was too young to enlist on my own—I was only seventeen years old—so my parents had to sign waivers for me. Confusion and fear filled my mother's eyes as I tried to explain my rationale for joining. She didn't like the idea one bit, knowing it would mean that at any time, her only son could be called to go to war, but neither did she prevent me from enlisting; maybe she, too, knew I needed a new direction.

Soon enough, the time to start basic training arrived. My family and I spent the night in a New Orleans hotel close to my deployment location; we had a wonderful time reminiscing and laughing. I knew my parents were concerned for me, but I could also see the pride in their eyes too.

Bright and early the next morning, I was on my way to Fort Leonard Wood, located in the Missouri Ozarks. The other recruits and I took a plane most of the way, then transferred to a bus. The moment the bus arrived at the base, I truly knew that I was now in the US Army. Our drill sergeant immediately boarded the bus and ordered us to get off the bus, get our luggage, and form a line. We had three minutes to comply.

The other recruits and I shuffled off the bus, grabbed our things, and formed a line. We thought we had made a good enough time, but we were also thinking like civilians. The drill sergeant immediately forced us to start over, barking at us all the while. After about ten tries, I was sure I had made a huge mistake in joining the military. I kept this thought to myself, though, because I knew there would be consequences for complaints. In all, it took us about twenty tries before we figured out a way to get off the bus and into formation within 180 seconds. At first, the other recruits and I had been angry because we felt we were given an impossible task. But we discovered that with determination and cooperation, we could do it.

That first day seemed to never end. We pounded out countless push-ups, completed mountains of paperwork, and waded through the piles of standard-issue gear and supplies. As evening came, we were exhausted but were not granted permission to sleep. During a lecture, I nodded off—and got caught. My punishment was push-ups until I almost vomited. At the time, I thought I was being tortured, but now I know this type of discipline was necessary to break me out of my civilian mind-set and strengthen both my mind and body.

Frustratingly, I still found myself in trouble during basic training. The military was supposed to be a way for me to escape my problems, but I only found more. I didn't yet know how to put my ego aside for a greater purpose. I had a strong sense of individuality and was taught to make my voice heard, both of which were antithetical to army life.

One of the first instances of getting in trouble came in my second or third week of basic training, when my drill sergeant noticed that I wasn't shaving. My teenage face was not growing hair at this point, so I always skipped the step of shaving in the morning. My drill sergeant ordered me to shave, telling me we were one unit and needed to stay in one accord. He said that I needed to take away my sense of self and shave with my fellow soldiers, even if there was no hair on my face to be removed.

My ethos of not snitching, which was ingrained in me from childhood, also complicated my life in the military. For example, I had knowledge of two soldiers, a man and woman, who were in a relationship that was inappropriate by military standards. I didn't bring this to my superiors' attention because I felt it was none of my business. But later, when the couple's secret was exposed, I was stripped of my rank because I hadn't reported their relationship. I lost time, pay, and status within my unit, even though I hadn't actually been involved in their activities in any way. On top of all that, I was placed on hard duty and had my telephone privileges revoked. I was allowed one call before I lost my phone privileges. I was ashamed to tell my mother that she wouldn't be hearing from me for a good long while.

The military taught me to think differently as the training continued day after day. I was soon in the best shape of my life, and my mind and body were becoming disciplined and regimented. In civilian life, I had seen guns: their purpose was to harm. In the military, there were no guns—only weapons—and weapons were solely for defense or protection. Previously, I had learned "many shots, many kills," but the basic training taught me a different line of defense, "one shot, two kills." With this mind-set, I was taught that I'd be able to protect my country and fellow soldiers.

While in the military, the special bond that I had with my baby sister grew stronger. I would send money home to buy her clothes and help get her prepared for the next school year. We would talk as often as we could. She was the best part of calling home for me, and we kept nothing from each other. Our discussions were the calming force that I needed during my times of turmoil.

When it was time to graduate, I didn't want my parents to come to the ceremony. Although my father's foreman position meant we were financially far more stable than ever before, money was still tight, and I didn't want them spending money on travel. I thought about paying their way, but the military salary I had told my parents about was heavily supplemented with my saved drug money; as much as I wanted to, I couldn't justify bringing them to the ceremony with dirty money.

I graduated with good marks both academically and physically. I was skilled with my rifle and in hand-to-hand combat techniques. Most importantly, I now felt in control of my actions. My quick temper, angst, and lack of self-control were replaced with calm and mature behavior. I was confident and disciplined in my emotions. I felt honored to be a soldier in the US armed forces and felt pride when I put on my uniform. The medical field was where I wanted to do my part, so I enrolled in the Advanced Individual Training (AIT) program to become a medical specialist. This is where I felt I could be of best use as a soldier while also pursuing medicine as a career and dedicating myself to the health and well-being of others.

My AIT training was at Fort Sam Houston in San Antonio, Texas, where I was trained as a 91 Bravo, a medical specialist/combat medic. Before I shipped out for San Antonio, I figured I'd be in a small hospital assisting with the medical care of soldiers. However, I was either confused or somehow misinformed by my recruiter. The hospital I had pictured didn't exist, and instead, I found myself being trained as a front-line medic. There was a combat element, too. Front-line medics could be called on at any time to fight with the infantry unit, so 91 Bravos were also trained in hand-to-hand combat.

Over my sixteen weeks in AIT, I was taught to treat acute medical issues that were likely to be seen on the battlefield. I assessed soldiers who were suffering from dehydration, broken bones, gunshot wounds, or other injuries. I learned basic medical skills and became a first line of defense against potentially life-threatening injuries. More importantly, I learned to stay calm and make critical patient assessments even under the most strenuous circumstances—in fact, I learned how to channel that stress and perform even better under pressure.

Without my military training, I could not have become the doctor I am today. While performing surgery, the complications or emergencies that can arise do not agitate me in the same way they sometimes seem to affect my colleagues. I can control my anxiety and focus more easily. Just as importantly, I can help my colleagues remain calm and focused as well. The ability to maintain a clear mind and a strong resolve during intense situations is the most valuable attribute I gained from the military. I am proud of my service and thankful for the lessons I learned.

After finishing my military duty, I signed up for the US Army Reserve and reentered Xavier University. My training had given me real-world experience in the medical field and had refortified my desire to become a doctor.

Unfortunately, being back in New Orleans proved to be a real challenge for me. The army had taught me a lot, but the reality was that I hadn't been away from New Orleans for very long. Maybe my few months away from home simply wasn't enough time to bring about the change I truly wanted for myself. I was now back in the very environment I had escaped from, and I reverted back to many of my old ways. I started partying and smoking marijuana again. I didn't start moving drugs myself, but I was still connected to the hustler life. Some friends whom I had introduced to the drug game before going into basic training had built themselves into high-level suppliers while I was away. They were now dealing thousands of dollars' worth of drugs, and merely knowing about their enterprise made me a part of their world, whether I liked it or not.

It's difficult to explain just how hard it is to remove negativity from your life. I battled with my conscience telling me one thing while my actions demonstrated another. I found it impossible to turn my back on my friends, even though I knew they were up to no good. I was being sucked right back into a life I'd tried so desperately to put behind me. Life was a puzzle for me, but I always wanted to do better.

October 13, 1996, is a date I will never forget. This is the day when my cousin Wayne was shot nine times by his friend over drugs. My cousin, whom I considered a brother and loved dearly, was gone at the young age of twenty-one.

My cousin was older than me and always had big ideas of success. He'd always been a role model for me and my other cousins. He was talented, and his heart was pure. I was the one who introduced my cousin to the fast life of violence and selling drugs. When I started selling crack, I would discuss that with him, and soon he started selling marijuana, going quickly from selling small amounts to large quantities. It consumed me with guilt that he was killed over something I had introduced to him. I had never felt pain like this before. Grief filled my entire body until I felt I would burst. My heart broke as I imagined the thoughts running through my cousin's mind as he saw his friend raise that gun, and I was haunted by the terror he must have surely faced in knowing his last moments were upon him. I was plagued by the betrayal and hurt he most certainly felt as his last breath approached. I felt all the more responsible for his death because I'd told my cousin many times to watch this friend closely. But my cousin had a heart of forgiveness—he never understood that this wasn't how things worked on the streets.

Guilt consumed me as if I had pulled that trigger myself. My cousin had begun dealing because of my influence. My mind kept scrolling back to our childhood. Wayne had always been like an older brother to me. When we were young, I was sure he could do anything in the world. He taught me and my other cousins to ride horses, rope pigs, light bonfires, build boats, and camp in the woods. Repairing things came naturally to him, and it seemed to us that he could fix anything—furniture, upholstery, new cars, classic cars. Wayne wanted to be a truck driver, and so I kept thinking about how, as a child, he would transform my bed into an eighteen-wheel semi using pillows and blankets. The two of us would sit there, bouncing up and down as if we were on a bumpy country road. Wayne always added sound effects; he would imitate the rumble of the Jake brake, "honk" the ear-splitting air horn, and make the whizzing sounds of cars passing by. It seemed so real, we could almost feel the wind on our faces.

And now, he was gone.

If I hadn't brought him into the game, he never would've gotten anywhere near that life. I had never thought about how my actions would affect others, nor did I ever truly believe that anyone in my family might be hurt, let alone murdered. I was weighted by immense remorse when I looked into the beautiful eyes of his now-fatherless twins.

Anger, hopelessness, guilt, grief—my emotions ran across an entire spectrum of darkness. I went into a deep depression and became reckless and even combative. All of the discipline I'd learned in the army dissolved. I had little control over my emotions. About a week after my cousin's funeral, some friends and I were in a club when, in the shuffle, my friend bumped into another person. I lashed out explosively. The next thing I knew, the man drew a gun on me. I should have been terrified, but as I looked down the barrel of that pistol, all I wanted was for him to pull the trigger. I wanted to pay for my wrongdoing. I trash-talked and egged the man on, saying everything I could to insult him. I felt no fear—just acceptance of my penance. Not one soul in the club intervened. In fact, the crowd around us had backed away and created a clear path for this man's bullet.

I have no idea why that man didn't take my life. Perhaps it was only by the grace of God that I was spared. At the time, however, I felt very differently. That evening, I cried in anger to God, asking why my life hadn't ended. I no longer wanted to feel the pain, no longer wanted the immense burden of this guilt. I no longer wanted to live.

I was in a total free fall. I began losing weight rapidly, and my grades at Xavier suffered to the point where I was put on academic probation. My family and childhood friends offered me extraordinary support and showed me kindness and love, none more than the brother of my murdered cousin. Yet for all their solace, I couldn't rid myself of my guilt. No contrition seemed enough. My cousin's death cast a pall over my life—one that I felt I deserved.

By His mercy, it was God who saved me, although He didn't answer my prayers in the way I thought He would. He didn't punish me, but instead, He opened my heart and gave me clarity. He revealed to me it was time to start a new life, and He gave me the resolve and strength I had been lacking for so long. It was time to be free of the streets and the pain that came with that life, to put all drugs and drug associations behind me. I would not ignore this blessing, and I resolved that I would lead an upright life, no matter what.

God knew that I needed to be tested if I were truly going to change my life—He knew that if the road were too easy, I would falter and return to my old ways yet again. This is why, soon after I vowed to change my life, I went to jail for a crime I didn't commit.

My baby sister and I were at my parents' house, where we were talking about my life-changing resolve and our dreams for her future success. The moment was so intimate that we both came close to tears. To this day, it remains as one of our deepest bonding moments.

A pounding knock at the door interrupted our conversation. I peeked out the window and saw two men in suits. Trembling, my sister opened the door while I hid because I knew that the only person they would be looking for would be me. I felt like maybe my past actions were catching up with me. I saw the fear in her eyes as the detectives announced that there was a warrant for my arrest. Out of love and fear, my baby sister lied and told them she didn't know where to find me. I immediately felt awful for placing my sister in a situation where she felt she needed to deceive the police for me. After the detectives left, I apologized repeatedly and begged for her forgiveness.

Obsessively, I began racking my brain for the cause of the warrant. So many possible events crossed my mind—I'd done so many stupid, foolish things that it was hard to narrow down the possibilities. I was all but paralyzed with fear: now that I had pledged to change my life, my actions were catching up with me. I called anyone who might have some insight into the warrant and began scouring the news for tips. When a reporter on TV recounted the story of a murdered police officer, the blood froze in my veins: I recognized the officer because I had recently had an encounter with him.

Several weeks earlier, this particular police officer had pulled me over and detained me for turning a corner too quickly. When he roughly pushed me against the hood of his hot car, the heat caused me to jerk away, and he immediately struck me on the back with his billy club. The pain was blinding, but I managed to control my anger; instead of fighting back, I clenched my teeth and listened while he gave me a pointless lecture on safe driving before he reluctantly let me go. Later, my mother told me to report the assault—the bruises on my back were evidence—but I never did. For one thing, I wanted to keep my name out of the legal system, but I also feared retaliation from the New Orleans police department, which everyone knew had a long history of corruption and racial profiling.[17] Now, this same police officer was dead. I was sure this was why the detectives were hunting me. I figured my life was over.

I had promised my sister that I would make things right, so I drove to the sheriff's department and turned myself in. I was brought into an interrogation room, where the conversation started out friendly enough. I was asked about some people—none of whom I knew—and about my whereabouts on a certain day. I answered all of their questions honestly, but the police must have thought I was withholding information because our conversation began to intensify. While I was trying to understand where their line of questioning was leading, I began asking God for clarity of thought.

Finally, one of the officers pulled out a logbook of tickets and accused me of never paying them, even though I was confident that those tickets were fully paid. I'd given the money for the fines to my friend's girlfriend who worked at the courthouse. The next thing I knew, a detective walked into the room: "You have the right to remain silent..." I knew I was powerless to stop whatever was about to happen next.

After reciting my Miranda rights, the detective informed me that he was taking me to holding. I was truly confused, and I asked the detective if I could speak with him privately before he transferred me. I told him about my military service, my current enrollment in Xavier University, and my plans to become a physician. I spoke of my life-changing transformation and my trustworthiness. I admitted my concern about how the people outside the police precinct would view me if they saw me in restraints, and I requested that the detective not handcuff me for the walk to the car.

Surprisingly, the officer complied with my request. We had a nice conversation on the drive to the jail, and I will always appreciate his professionalism and respect toward me as a human being. The officer did have to handcuff me for the walk into holding, and I understood. I didn't want him to break protocol for me.

17 Among other sources, supporting information can be found by visiting the websites of CNN at http://www.cnn.com/2011/US/03/17/louisiana.new.orleans.police/index.html, the US Department of Justice at https://www.justice.gov/sites/default/files/crt/legacy/2011/03/17/nopd_report.pdf, and *The Times-Picayune* at http://www.nola.com/crime/index.ssf/2016/08/nopd_stop_search_data_black_wh.htm.

I was placed into a holding cell. To my surprise, the brother of an old friend was in the cell too. This man was broken. He was dirty, he reeked, and he was clearly an addict. I began to minister to him, and we talked about the old days. I spoke of God and how He spared me from street life. I told this poor man how Jesus could save him too. I literally gave him the shirt off my back because he had nothing, and I wanted to do what I thought Jesus would do.

After a full investigation, I was released from jail a couple days later with only fines and community service. Apparently, the woman who had promised to pay my tickets had pocketed the money for herself, which had resulted in the warrant for my arrest. There were many times previously when I should have been incarcerated. I decided to use being locked up for such a minor offense as a learning experience. I did feel some bitterness, and within that bitterness was the temptation to turn back to my old ways. However, I found in myself the strength that God had given to me, and I accepted this experience as a test of His design.

I wanted to share my new peace with my friends and family. Shortly afterward, I had the opportunity to minister to an old friend who had spent ten years in prison. I encouraged him to pray and come to church with me. I testified on the goodness of God and Christ's acceptance of all who believe in Him—no matter how bad or unforgivable we may think we are. My friend was very receptive and started turning his life around. But tragically, just as he was beginning to make a way for himself, he was murdered. I can still see him lying motionless on the cold ground.

I spoke at my friend's funeral. I talked about his new outlook on life and his path with Christ. Even though he'd found himself in the wrong place at the wrong time, we could take comfort because he was in the right place now. I continue to be comforted in knowing I will see my friend again one day.

Once I made a concerted effort in my life, one of the things I knew I had to do to truly make things right was to help the older brother of my murdered cousin through his hard times, especially since he had been present at the time of Wayne's death. In my heart, it felt paramount that I create a whole new relationship with him so that I could help ease the void in his life. I wanted to be a source of comfort, a listening ear, and a brother to him. Ever since, my relationship with him has been an ongoing blessing and a vital part of my own healing process. Through this relationship, we have continued to show support and love to each other not only as cousins, but as brothers. His poise and kindness continue to be an inspiration to me.

Even though my drug-dealing days were over, I still had some saved drug money that I needed to free myself from. I wouldn't spend a dime of it on myself. I knew if I did, I wouldn't be blessed. I couldn't give any of the money to my mother because she wouldn't want any part of my sinful earnings. Shameful of my actions, I couldn't even give the money to the church. I felt giving the church unclean money would be blasphemy against God, who had delivered me and spared my life. It would take me a few years, but I did slowly manage to get rid of all that money. I gave it to the homeless, to those whom I saw struggling, and to various charity organizations.

CHAPTER 19

Higher Education

I WENT BACK TO XAVIER University with a renewed determination to finish my degree and further my career. Now, after all I'd been through since returning from the military, I had truly put my past behind me. I was *done* with drugs. I was filled with a presaged dread telling me that I'd die within twenty-four hours if I ever touched drugs again. I believed in my heart that I was spared so that I could get my education and ultimately help others. My coauthors, Max Madhere and Pierre Johnson, were truly a gift. I saw myself in them but in a better, cleaner form. Here I saw two cool guys studying and working toward their goals. They showed me that utilizing my intelligence was also cool and that there were many worthy things to strive for in life, rather than wasting my promise on the foolishness and negativity I had allowed myself to fall into. I'd never met two more genuine young men in my life.

Xavier's premed curriculum was brimming with challenges for all three of us. We began studying together every day, and we held one another up as each new challenge presented itself. Because I'm a little bit older than Max and Pierre, I would like to think I was able to offer them some advice along the way, but truly, it was the two of them who kept me moving toward a better life for myself. Their faith in me and our commitment to succeeding together healed the last of the anger I had been carrying since I was a child. From the moment I met them to this very day, I've never gotten near street life again.

The three of us took advantage of every bit of the extraordinary support Xavier's premed office offered. We all looked up to Dr. Carmichael, the medical program director; he was always available to answer students' questions and had a style of teaching that made learning easier. He pushed us to embrace the challenges we faced as premedical students and to overcome those challenges. He gave us all confidence, reminding us almost every day that there was nothing we couldn't overcome with hard work.

We weren't great students academically, but no one could match us for sheer effort. The three of us spent many a late night in the library, and we often studied to the point of exhaustion. To counter this, we came up with a power-nap system. One of us would doze off for a few minutes while the other two continued studying. We did this round-robin style so that each of us could get the rest we needed to stay focused without losing too much time.

I stayed enrolled at Xavier, without any more interruptions, until I graduated. During that last year of college, the Medical College Admission Test (MCAT) proved to be a real challenge for me, so I began thinking of other paths to accomplish my goal of becoming a physician. I had taken a number of prep courses for the MCAT—I was certainly prepared in terms of knowledge—but my standardized-test-taking skills were not strong, and ultimately, my MCAT score remained unimpressive. By the end of the year, my cumulative GPA, too, wasn't medical-school-acceptance level. My false start and early academic probation took their toll on my overall average. Getting into medical school would require an interim step, so I decided to enroll in Tulane University's graduate program. I hoped that a master's degree in public health would make me more attractive to medical schools.

The masters of public health program at Tulane offered me the opportunity to strengthen my study skills and reinforce my medical and scientific knowledge. By now, I knew how imperative it was to keep my GPA at the top of the class, so I rededicated my academic focus. Max and Pierre, along with Xavier's premed office, had drilled good study habits into me until they had become second nature. I now had confidence that my study skills were ready for graduate-level demands. My course of study was in tropical medicine and parasitology, which meant that I could continue forward with my studies in disease pathology while also opening up my knowledge base regarding insect and parasite infections specifically. Pursuing a degree in public health also gave me a viable backup plan in case all else failed and I didn't get into medical school. If I couldn't become a doctor, then at least I could help improve people's health in other ways.

Tulane's graduate program required one and a half years of study. When choosing my graduate school, I knew I wanted to stay in New Orleans for both personal and financial reasons. In-state tuition rates and Louisiana-specific grants were major considerations, but they almost paled in comparison with my real reason for staying in New Orleans. Now that I was a few years older, I understood that running away from my life, as I had done when I joined the military, would never be a real solution. God wanted me to face any obstacles in my life head-on while turning to Him for guidance and deliverance. Additionally, I didn't relish the idea of leaving my family, as I was only now starting to build relationships with them as a Christian adult.

The chair of my department understood my ultimate goal of becoming a physician. He did everything he could to help me develop into a well-rounded graduate student who would be attractive to medical schools. Because Tulane's public health program wasn't affiliated with a hospital, I wouldn't be able to do any clinical work, but my chair did offer me an alternate path that would showcase my commitment to preventative care. Oddly enough, this is how I found myself wading through Louisiana's wetlands and bayous, chasing after mosquitoes.

At that time, the West Nile virus, which is most commonly spread to humans through mosquito bites, had been introduced to the United States only a few years earlier.[18] Infections in the United States were particularly pernicious, and Louisiana responded to this serious public health risk through the Louisiana Mosquito Abatement Program. My job was to visit different parishes in the state, capture mosquito samples, then analyze the different diseases they carried. The program would then encourage preventative measures in high-risk areas, as well as recommend the safest and most effective pesticides for hyperlocal use. I enjoyed working in the lab and analyzing specimens, but sometimes, working with the abatement program seemed about as far away from medicine as I could possibly get—the scrubs and white lab coats I pictured myself wearing one day had been replaced by waders and overalls. The abatement program

18 Supporting information can be found by visiting the World Health Organization website at http://www.who.int/mediacentre/factsheets/fs354/en/.

was a wonderful opportunity with a strong community-service element that I remember fondly, and I did gain some solid fieldwork skills, but I was far more interested in human beings than bugs.

I stayed in close contact with Max and Pierre while in graduate school. They had both been accepted into a premed preparatory program at Southern Illinois University, where they were working to improve their MCAT scores. At times, I wished I was with them, but I hadn't been accepted into the program. When talking to my two brothers, it seemed like they devoted 100 percent of their time to studying, and that made me want to focus even more time on my own studies. It's difficult to describe the way the three of us fed off one another, but our brotherhood was vital to my success. Even though our relationship had become a long-distance one, they helped motivate me during my time at Tulane and kept me focused on my ultimate goal.

I graduated from Tulane in 2003. In between completing my master's program and beginning medical school, I started teaching high school chemistry. Working with urban and inner-city kids who were experiencing some of the same challenges I faced as a teen was one of the most rewarding periods of my life. So much of my past life was plagued with darkness and fatuity. I now had the opportunity to be a positive influence in the lives of young people.

On the first day in the classroom, I spent a large portion of the day explaining rules and expectations for the school year. In one of my classes, a student was immediately disruptive. He was disrespectful to both me and the entire class. He refused to listen to anything I said, bragged about his self-appointed title of a fighter, and proclaimed that he and his boys ruled the school.

This student continued to be disruptive. By day three, I was ready to break, but there was a little too much of my former self in this young man. I resolved not to expel him from my class. Expelling him wouldn't solve the underlying problem, and I knew it. I could see "Lil Joe" in his angry and defiant expression. If I didn't reach this kid, it was possible that no one ever would. Without intervention, this student surely would become another casualty of street life.

After a couple of weeks, I decided to talk to the young man privately. There was no way he was going to sit through a typical condescending lecture about self-improvement and achievement; I knew I needed a different approach to get his attention. One afternoon, I asked him to come to the back room, with the full knowledge that what I was about to do could result in my being fired. But I was so concerned about this young man that it was a risk worth taking.

I grabbed his shirt collar and began to pour my heart out. I told him that I had been just like him and that I had already gone down the road he was traveling. I didn't hold back anything. I laid bare all the anguish, fear, and uncertainty that came with my street life. I told him of the friends and family I had lost and of all my old friends who were rotting away in jail cells. Most of all, I told him that I refused to let him make the same mistakes because I cared about him.

That conversation changed this student's life. Perhaps all he needed was someone to believe in him, much like I did. He began taking school seriously and earned high marks in my class. He even stayed late after class and helped me tutor his fellow classmates. His new attitude and resolve were so strong that he paved the way for other struggling students. By committing to his own achievement, he made it "cool" for other students to seek help, which allowed me to mentor them too.

I enjoyed sharing my history with every student I mentored, and I strived to teach all of my students that they could achieve any goal regardless of their personal situations. Many of my students felt I was one of the few people who truly cared about them, which both elated and saddened me. At the end of the year, my students' grief weighed heavily on me when I announced I would be leaving to go to medical school. I hated to leave these kids behind, but I was also excited about moving on with my career. I wouldn't be able to actively mentor and guide my students any longer, but soon, if I studied hard, I knew I'd be able to help many, many others.

I was proud, a few years later, to help two of my students enroll in my alma mater, Xavier University. In that moment, I felt I had fulfilled my purpose as a teacher. I knew Xavier would devote every resource available to helping them achieve their own dreams, and I was grateful to have played a small part in that.

CHAPTER 20

Balancing Act

FATHERHOOD. WHAT A SCARY THING. I had first met my girlfriend—who is today my wife—at Xavier. She was a speech pathology major, and we had met on campus once or twice, but we didn't begin dating until after I'd graduated from Tulane. The moment my girlfriend told me she was pregnant, I was determined to be with her every step of the way, despite the judgment I knew we would face from both our families for not being wed.

We also knew we had another challenge to face. My girlfriend's type I diabetes meant that we would have to work hard to achieve normal glucose levels throughout her pregnancy. We followed every instruction our doctor gave us and met every recommended metric. In a way, my girlfriend was my very first patient. I worked with her day and night to help monitor and control her blood glucose. When we reached the end of her pregnancy without a single diabetic incident, we thought we had beaten all the odds.

However, our delivery day was very different from the joyous occasion we were expecting. Because of my girlfriend's diabetes, our doctor recommended an induced labor, which could be monitored closely. We arrived at the hospital with everything prepared. My girlfriend had picked out a beautiful nightgown for herself, and we had a handsome little outfit ready for my son to wear when he arrived into the world. Members from both of our families gathered to support us on this momentous occasion. We had already decided to name our son Joseph III, and I was anxious and excited to meet this new version of myself.

The staff administered medication to my girlfriend to induce labor and help bring on contractions. Soon, her contractions became regular, at which point the doctor broke her water. In between her increasingly intense contractions, we enjoyed listening to our son's heartbeat on the fetal monitor. We had every reason to believe that this would be a relatively routine birthing. How wrong we were.

What came next nearly broke me. My son's heartbeat slowed, and the precious beeps from the fetal monitor became farther and farther apart. The medical part of me understood what was happening, but as a father, I couldn't fathom the scene before me. A full emergency team had rushed into the room, and they were now performing a cesarean section. When they removed my son from the womb, he was pure blue and utterly lifeless. I watched with fear and helplessness as the medical team began resuscitation efforts. I can still hear them as they counted out the compressions, "And one, and two, and three, and four, and five..." I was rooted to the floor in utter horror. Mercifully, one of the hospital's nuns handed me a rosary. I prayed for my son like I had never prayed before.

The medical team rushed my son to another unit, and I could no longer see what was happening. My girlfriend, concerned that no one had handed her our new baby, anxiously asked what was happening. Because I felt it best to give her a moment of peace to recover, I lied and said our baby was doing just fine, that he just needed a little extra attention. I stayed with her until she was sent to recovery, then went to check on my son. My heart sunk straight into my stomach when I learned the medical team was having difficulty keeping his breathing steady, maintaining his body temperature, and elevating his low blood sugar level. Utter dismay flooded me when I learned that my son had endured over fifteen minutes of resuscitation efforts. What kind of a way was this to come into the world?

I returned to my girlfriend's bedside. In a moment when so much already seemed so lost, she began having eclamptic seizures, which caused her to slip into a coma. The hospital staff frantically took lifesaving measures, then immediately performed a computed tomography (CAT) scan of her brain. At that point, her kidneys and liver began shutting down, and most of her medications had to be discontinued to avoid life-threatening toxicity levels. Throughout the night, I remained glued to my girlfriend's bed in the intensive care unit (ICU), in fear for her life. I watched helplessly as her blood pressure continued to creep upward despite every available medical measure. I was terrified to leave her side and even more terrified of visiting my ailing son. I was so afraid we were going to lose him. This was the most desperate moment of my life; all was in the Lord's hands. All I could do was pray for His mercy.

By the third day, my son stabilized, and I was finally able to bring myself to visit him in the neonatal ICU. It broke my heart to see him—tubes were connected to him in every direction, and he was surrounded by monitors. As the tears fell from my eyes, I prayed fervently and asked God to touch my son, to heal him. I didn't stay in the neonatal ICU long. It just hurt too much. With all of my medical training, I understood how truly perilous my son's condition was—I simply knew too much. I returned to my girlfriend's bedside and watched her monitors again. Seeing her lying there almost lifeless was no easier.

My son's health continued to improve. The following day, I held him for the first time and was able to feed him. Pride, love, and hope swelled inside of me in that moment. I listened to my baby boy breathe and watched his little throat as he fed. His tiny toes, all curled up, were perfection incarnate. I marveled at how small he was in my hands.

My girlfriend was still in a coma on the sixth day, but I wanted my son to meet his mother. The hospital staff advised otherwise, but in my heart, I knew they needed to be together, if only for a few moments. I placed my tiny son on her chest so that they could feel each other's heartbeats. The sight of them together, both with tubes and monitors all around them, was at once horrifying and magical.

To this day, I believe my son's meeting his mother created a miracle. My prayers were answered the next day when my girlfriend awoke. She opened her eyes and immediately asked for JoJo. I knew then and there that our son had a nickname. One week later, I had the privilege of bringing my new family home from the hospital.

I had started researching medical schools when I was teaching high school. Given my subpar performance on the MCAT, I focused my search on foreign schools, many of which took a whole-applicant approach to admissions. Not long after the birth of JoJo, I began applying to medical schools and was accepted to several institutions. I decided on Saint Matthew's University School of Medicine in the Cayman Islands.

Going abroad for medical school was a huge decision because it meant leaving my girlfriend and infant son. My girlfriend was very supportive of my decision. She knew the vision I had for myself and our family. I desperately wanted her and JoJo to come with me, but obtaining a work visa for her would've been almost impossible, and she already had a good job as well as family support in New Orleans. After several long discussions, we both concluded that living apart was the best decision for our family.

I chose Saint Matthew's for several reasons. First, the Cayman Islands have a culture and economy not dissimilar from those of the United States, English is the predominant language, and the dollar is accepted almost everywhere. Second, Saint Matthew's had a strong medical program that included US licensure, and my requisite two years of clinical study would be at a US hospital. Lastly, flights from the Cayman Islands were priced fairly reasonably, and I was determined to see my family as often as I could.

Saint Matthew's did have its drawbacks. Aside from being away from my family, the class and clinical structures of Caribbean medical schools were different from those in the United States, and I knew this would require some adjustment. There was a fair amount of risk involved, too, since Saint Matthew's placed only about 60 percent of its medical students in residency programs—far lower than the average placements of US schools. A good part of the reason for this low placement rate was because Saint Matthew's didn't focus on standardized test prep, which meant that many students didn't pass Step 1 of United States Medical Licensing Examination (USMLE). Since standardized tests were always my biggest educational challenge, this was a major concern. All the more daunting was knowing that my USMLE Step 1 score would have to be exceedingly high in order to make myself more attractive than residency candidates from US schools. Even so, I made up in my mind that I wasn't going to be in the 40 percent of medical students who didn't achieve residency placement. I had been through too much with the birth of my son, and now it was time to push forward and set myself on the road to being the father, provider, and doctor I knew I could be.

When I arrived on Grand Cayman Island, I felt in my gut that I was in an entirely different world. I was amazed at the beautiful landscape, the crystal-clear water, and the delicious Caribbean foods. The island was so breathtaking that I had to vow to myself to ignore its beauties and focus on my studies—my time there could not be an extended vacation. In order to finish medical school on time, I would need to spend my first two years of the program focused on studying and nothing else.

I was more than eager to dive into my studies. Medical school was a fresh start in so many ways, and a part of me was awestruck by the possibilities to come. From this point forward, I knew my previous grades—both good and bad—no longer mattered. The MCAT was now irrelevant, and all of my missteps and lack of focus were behind me. I was now ready to give everything I had to earning my MD, and I felt as if I were in control of my destiny for the very first time.

Medical school was bursting with challenges. The constant reading and studying were trying, but even more difficult was the way classes were structured. All of my classes were lectures, with a test in each at least once a week. There was little one-on-one teaching, and I almost never spoke directly to my professors. Almost immediately, I knew that self-teaching and major self-discipline would be necessary. Unlike Xavier, Saint Matthew's offered almost no academic support system for struggling students. There were no supplementary classes, no true counselors, and definitely no tutoring system. Passing or failing was solely up to me.

I was also one of the very few black students in the program, and none of the faculty was of African descent either. I saw few people who looked like me and even fewer who I felt could relate to me or had experienced some of the same struggles. I knew my path to medical school had been a nontraditional one, but I had hoped to find someone who understood, endemically, my background and challenges.

I was not without good company, however. I had met Jeet and Ronak my first day on the island. They had traveled to Saint Matthew's from Houston. They were both of Indian descent and spoke Hindi at home. Their culture was different from mine, and their favorite foods were different from mine, but our goals were the same. We respected one another's cultures and formed a friendship through our shared goals. Later, Ronak would become my roommate. The three of us were a big source of support for one another during our first two years of medical school. We spent countless hours studying together.

I was blessed in that I was able to adapt to my new environment, but even with Ronak and Jeet's friendship, the isolation made my time in medical school all the more difficult. My separation from my family seemed that much more acute. I had all these plans for being a father, yet now I was a thousand miles away from my son. My girlfriend and I did our best to stay connected as a family during my absence, and webcams became our creative way of eating dinner together. Even with my girlfriend's extraordinary support, I would still weep in private because I missed my son and was mourning my lost moments with him. I feared that JoJo, as he grew older, wouldn't understand my reasons for being away and would always resent me on some level.

My path in medical school changed in a big way after only a few weeks at Saint Matthew's. Grand Cayman Island was in the path of a huge hurricane, which forced us to evacuate to Miami. After only a few days in Florida, we were told that Saint Matthew's had been heavily damaged by the storm, and we couldn't return to campus. Dismay and panic hit me. I didn't know if I'd be able to continue my schooling. What would happen to my career? How would I provide for my family? Would I need to start the application process all over again and begin at another school?

Amid all these questions, the hurricane did have one positive, personally speaking: I was able to fly home for JoJo's first birthday. The party's theme was "Lightning McQueen," and we invited a horde of children to celebrate with us. When we brought out the cake and sang "Happy Birthday," JoJo tried very hard to blow out the candle, but he finally gave up and instead grabbed two huge fistfuls of cake. The moment the sticky-sweet icing touched his tongue, we all knew it was the best thing he had ever tasted. The pure joy on his face was priceless. Even with all the unanswered questions about my schooling hanging over my head, it meant the world to me to witness this moment.

A few days after the party, Saint Matthew's sent out a memo stating that all medical students would be relocated to the school's Maine campus, which was usually reserved for students in their combined master's/MD program. I was relieved that I would be able to continue my studies with less than a month's interruption and could still graduate on time. Relocating to the Maine campus also meant that flights home would be less expensive, a bit shorter, and without the hassle of international travel.

I never knew so much snow existed. Gone were the Caribbean breezes, tropical weather, and sunny skies. On the bright side, also eliminated were all the temptations of Grand Cayman Island: Maine's gray skies and biting cold kept me to my studies. Even though New England's culture was very different from that of New Orleans, being in my home country helped a little with the loneliness.

Like the island campus, Saint Mathew's in Maine offered almost no supplemental support. I was blessed that I had made friends who understood the importance of mastering the coursework, but it's difficult to express how stressful and isolating it was not to have resources to turn to when I didn't understand a concept or was struggling with a particular topic. I remained in close contact with Max and Pierre during this time. They empathized with my frustrations and helped me all they could, even though they were both overwhelmed with their own challenges in medical school.

I spent two semesters in Maine before Saint Matthew's island campus reopened. I flew back to Grand Cayman Island and ultimately completed my first two years of medical school with a high GPA. In addition to my classes, much of my second year was focused on preparing for the USMLE Step 1, which is by far the most difficult of the three USMLE tests. Again, I was blessed. A few of my friends in the program were as focused as I was on early exam prep. Like I had done with Max and Pierre during our MCAT challenge, my friends and I formed study groups and pushed one another to work just that much harder. We took practice exams and enrolled in prep courses outside of Saint Matthew's to improve our test-taking skills. Yet, even with all my solid prep work, severe stress, anxiety, insomnia, and exhaustion plagued me as the day of the test approached.

I was confident in my knowledge base when I first took the USMLE Step 1, but unfortunately, knowledge wasn't enough—I failed by just two points. I was crushed. This was a true setback. It was paramount that my score be exceptional in order to achieve residency placement. True sadness and disappointment filled me. I felt like a failure and was afraid for both myself and the future of my family. I thought of giving up, but my beautiful son kept appearing in my mind. My baby boy was my new inspiration. He gave me the strength to persevere, and I knew in my heart that God had not brought me this far to have me fail. Deep down, I knew success was part of a greater plan for me—I only needed to follow His guidance to find the right path.

That path started with a phone call. After receiving my disappointing exam results, I called Pierre, who was studying at the University of Illinois, for support. He, too, had failed the USMLE by a tiny margin. Neither of us was going to give up. The next thing I knew, I found myself in Peoria, where Pierre and I embarked on a self-made, month-long crash-course focused on rigorous study and prayer. I never hit the books so hard in my life—we studied up to sixteen hours a day. Having my brother by my side pushed me all the more. I knew we could both pass our exams if we remained united in our goals and faith.

With God's mercy and guidance, my second attempt at the USMLE Step 1 was successful, and I passed with high marks. The first hurdle to licensing was behind me. Now I could focus on the next step of medical school: two years of clinical clerkships.

In the Caribbean system, students do all of their basic science studies in the first two years of school, with the last two years being clinical study at various US hospitals. This is part of the reason why many Caribbean students take a little longer to finish their schooling; available clinical clerkships don't always line up with the academic calendar of Caribbean schools. This was yet another drawback of attending Saint Matthew's, as it took me a little over four years to finish my schooling.

My first clinical rotations were in New York City at the Wyckoff Medical Center in Brooklyn. Now I would have the opportunity to do hands-on work with patients. Third-year medical students had limited clinical responsibilities; we were monitored closely for the sake of patient safety. For the first time, I had real patients in my care. I did all I could to learn about their conditions and provide for their well-being.

New York City, with its incredible diversity, proved to be a benison to my clerkship. The hospital staff, and my patients, came from all over the world and from every walk of life. I no longer felt so isolated. Working with such a heterogeneous population helped me to focus on my clinical responsibilities. It also freed me from some of the inherent prejudices that young black male doctors can face. Few people in Brooklyn gave a thought to the color of my skin. Instead, they focused on my abilities as a third-year student and my promise as a doctor. I did most of my third and fourth years at the Wyckoff Medical Center before transferring to the Tulane Medical Center. At Tulane, my rotations were focused on my chosen specialty, obstetrics and gynecology.

Just as I was finishing up the last few months of my clerkships, I received some blessed, but frightening, news: my girlfriend was pregnant with our second child. I was overjoyed by the idea of having another little life to care for but also terribly afraid that this pregnancy would again result in serious health risks for both my baby and my girlfriend.

My fears were unfounded. God answered our prayers and allayed our fears by blessing us with a complication-free pregnancy and birth. Miguel, our seven-pound miracle, was born in the spring of 2009. My second son was the picture of health, and my girlfriend didn't face a single undue complication during labor.

CHAPTER 21

Stepping into My Purpose

I PASSED THE USMLE STEP 2 and graduated from medical school in 2008. With my MD complete, I began the search for a residency program in my chosen area of specialization. I had become attracted to obstetrics and gynecology as a medical student, and as I moved through my clinical rotations, I realized that ob-gyn truly was the specialty in my heart. Surgery had always been a passion of mine, and the variety of surgeries performed by an ob-gyn would wholly fulfill that passion. Having witnessed the birth of JoJo, and with Miguel due to arrive in early 2009, I knew that delivering children into the world would create a wonderful sense of fulfillment and joy both personally and professionally. Additionally, the opportunity to connect with my patients and their loved ones throughout the many different stages of life appealed to the strong commitment to community and family that my mother had instilled in me.

My passion to pursue obstetrics and gynecology had been shot down by many of my clerkship advisors because I had attended a Caribbean medical school. Ob-Gyn residencies are notoriously competitive, and they advised me to take an alternative route and pursue another field. But I had sacrificed far too much to achieve my medical degree. I had not worked so hard to compromise at that point. I went against all recommendations, and when match day arrived, I was focused on ob-gyn placements. All of my interviews went well, and I was sure I would match into a residency program.

Tulane Medical Center was my first choice of programs because I had graduated from that institution and had done part of my clinical training there. I also longed to be back in my home city of New Orleans, close to my family. I felt confident that my past mistakes were completely behind me and that no temptation from my past would be powerful enough to distract me from my career and family. However, returning home at that moment was not in God's plan for me. Instead, I was accepted into a program at Central Michigan University's College of Medicine hospital, my second-choice program.

I was elated. Not only had I found an ob-gyn residency, but being accepted into the program also meant that my time apart from my family had finally come to an end. My resident's salary meant that my family could move with me. The four of us relocated to Saginaw, Michigan—over a thousand miles from New Orleans—just months after Miguel was born.

As a new resident, I sometimes felt unsure about myself. This was the first time that patients were directly in my care, with only an attending physician overseeing me. In my heart, my earnest desire was to provide the very best possible care for my patients. Oddly enough, I never feared the many complications that could arise during treatment, but I was terrified that I might provide less-than-perfect care due to lack of experience. I shadowed senior residents to learn all I could from them, and I supplemented my long days in the hospital with study sessions at night. I would not fail those who entrusted their health to me.

My second year of residency was as much of a whirlwind as the first. In the midst of all this, my girlfriend and I sanctified our bond by pledging ourselves to each other in holy matrimony. Joy filled my heart as I watched my beautiful bride—the mother of my children and my longtime love—walk down the aisle. Our union would provide our sons with a sense of stability and impress upon them the importance of family.

When we returned from our honeymoon, my studying began anew as I prepared to take my final USMLE test. After passing this exam, I advanced to my final two years of residency. As I prepared to become a fully licensed physician, I turned a critical eye on my strengths and weaknesses as a doctor. I never wanted to encounter an ailment or medical procedure that I was unfamiliar with, never wanted a lack of training to impede patient care. Each night, I would drive home after clinic, have dinner with my family, then head back to the hospital to study in the medical library. The library staff came to know me well. I asked for material on all kinds of diseases, even those that were very rare. I would scour the articles they retrieved for me and continually expanded my knowledge base.

One of my most satisfying experiences as a third-year resident came not while on rounds but during a rare afternoon of leisure. That day, my friend and I had decided to spend the beautiful sunny day out on a nearby lake. We loaded our families into a motorboat and set out to enjoy the weather. Another boater in a sleek speedboat was zipping around the lake and enjoying the day as well. Suddenly, the boat hit a wave hard and was thrown into the air. The crash was so powerful that the boat split into pieces. I was sure there would be no survivors.

As we sped toward the wreck, I saw a body break the water's surface. We pulled in as close as we safely could, then my friend and I dove into the water to rescue the young man. He screamed in pain as we carefully swam him to our boat. His injuries were gory. I could see the terrified expressions on my children's faces.

I began to examine the young man from head to toe for injuries. There was a small cut on his head, but my biggest concern was the gash in his side, which was bleeding profusely. With the extremely limited resources available in our boat, all I could do was apply pressure to the gash and monitor this poor man for symptoms of life-threatening shock. This was enough to keep him alive until we reached the shore, where the paramedics were already waiting. When his mother arrived on the scene, her eyes revealed a mixture of fear and relief that I will never forget. She still sends me messages from time to time to thank me and to see how my family and I are faring. Somehow, I ended up at exactly the right place at the right time to save her son's life. I will forever be thankful that I was able to help this man.

My fourth year of residency was perhaps the most transformational of all my years of schooling. With only a year before I became a practicing ob-gyn, I devoted my residency's fourth year to shaping myself into the type of physician I truly wanted to be. I gave extra attention to improving my bedside manner and communicating with my patients; conveying respect, caring, and trust through my words became my main focus. I would listen carefully as my attendings counseled patients and their families, and I would even write down phrases that

I thought were well stated so that I could commit them to memory. Obstetrics and gynecology are deeply intimate fields. I wanted my patients not merely to trust my professional knowledge but to feel in their hearts how deeply I cared about their well-being.

One of the hardest realities of being a doctor is that we must sometimes tell our patients difficult news that comes with some tough choices. At times, delivering such news can be devastating. We must maintain our professionalism while deep down inside, our hearts are breaking. It's the most difficult part of the job for many of us. But my mentor, Dr. Littles—a renowned interventional radiologist—inspired me and guided me in finding ways of delivering necessary news with sensitivity, warmth, and respect. As I watched him and other attending physicians counsel patients who were facing dire circumstances, I learned how to bring my spirituality into my professional life. I would pray to God to use me as an instrument of healing, to help me find the right words in hard situations, and to accept that, truly, our lives are all in His hands.

As a way of using every last minute of my residency as a learning experience, I redoubled my clinical efforts. One of my attendings had advised me to approach every minor case as if it were something brand new. I took his insight to heart and followed his advice to the letter.

My attending's words proved to be prescient. A week or so afterward, I found myself unable to dilate the cervix of a patient who was undergoing a routine procedure. In that moment, I heard my attending's words resonate in my ear. I knew then that I would have to become a master of the "easy cases." For one thing, routine cases would always make up the majority of my patient load. But a far more important question loomed in my mind. Without this mastery, how could I ask the women I would treat to trust me as their doctor?

As strange as it may seem, in my fourth residency year, I was plagued once again by the exact same feeling I had when I started my residency. I never balked at the idea of having to make a life-or-death decision in a moment of crisis, but what truly scared me was not offering the very best possible treatment to my patients. Even as I worked to integrate my spirituality into patient care and communication, a part of me was always second-guessing my abilities.

Anxiety has no place in the operating room, so I actively worked to bring my soldier's training into my work. I began approaching each surgical case systematically, no matter how routine or complex the patient's needs. Even while my "civilian's mind" focused on treating my patients with compassion and kindness, my "soldier's mind" could approach a case with detachment and logic. Forcing myself back into the structured mind-set of my AIT training provided the last piece I needed to become a confident surgeon.

There was one case in particular where a patient in her early forties needed a large ovarian cyst removed. Her case was complicated because she had undergone several abdominal surgeries in the past. At our first consultation, I met her children; they were all respectful but also blissfully ignorant of how ill their mother really was. She was a single mother, and I could tell she was her children's entire world.

Even as my heart swelled for her three little angels, my soldier's mind began formulating a systematic plan for this patient's care. I tried to anticipate any complications I might face during her surgery. I read up on bowel anatomy and repair and modified her postoperative care plan to account for her previous surgeries. The surgery itself would be a longer one, up to four hours, and so it was crucial that I be able to minimize any stress to her intestines during the procedure. The night before her surgery, I was up so late planning and researching that I only found peace by meditating on the Serenity Prayer.

The surgery was challenging, just as I expected it to be. My surgical team and I found significant scar tissue that we weren't expecting, but I was able to remove these. Thanks in large part to my preparations, the rest of the surgery went fairly smoothly.

The last challenge of my residency was passing the first part of my ob-gyn board exams. With the written test fast approaching, I was highly motivated, and I once again found myself buried in exam prep for hours upon hours. Pierre and I, along with our friend Norman, would spend hours on the phone drilling one another. On test day, I felt—for the first time since I first entered medical school—truly prepared. By this point, standardized tests were no longer daunting. With experience, I had learned how to effectively navigate these exams because I knew what questions would be asked in each subject. As I walked into the exam room, I was eager for the challenge and even more eager for my hard-earned rewards.

I passed the exam with flying colors. With my first board exam now under my belt, it was time to start looking for a practice to join. I had a lot of ideas about where I would like to practice, but above all else, I wanted God to lead me to wherever He desired me to be. As I finished up the last months of my residency, I began interviewing at several different practices. In the end, I went back home to Louisiana.

I found a practice in Lake Charles, where I immediately felt at home. I had driven through Lake Charles many times on the highway, but this was my first time in the town itself. The folks I met during my interview were warm and welcoming, and the practice was located in a large women's health center with excellent facilities. Additionally, the position offered both autonomy as well as the potential for career growth. It was the perfect place to begin my career. I'd now be caring for the women of my home state while living only three hours away from New Orleans.

My family and I moved to Lake Charles. After eight years of medical training, part of me felt ready to join the medical group, but the idea of practicing medicine without my mentors to guide me was also a bit frightening. Half of me felt I was ready to take Lake Charles head-on, but the other half of me was humbled. The first day on the job, as I sat in my new office, I felt excited but also pensive. It was very similar to the feeling I had after my cousin was taken from this world. I began remembering all the steps and obstacles on my path: street life, the army, Xavier, Tulane, medical school, residency. I believe my sadness came because I felt like I didn't deserve to be so greatly blessed, or somehow, I would have to pay for the sins I had committed so long ago. After careful reflection and prayer, a true sense of joy and accomplishment broke through. I was now a practicing ob-gyn. I had achieved my goal. God had given me all that a man could ask for—a loving wife who had supported me through so much, two sons, and a job in my life's vocation. I truly believed that I had stepped into my purpose.

CHAPTER 22

Perceptions and Beyond

BECAUSE OF OUR PERCEIVED LACK of experience, inspiring patient trust immediately can be a challenge for young doctors—patients often want older doctors who have seen it all. As a young black doctor, I faced yet another obstacle: black men aren't "supposed to be" doctors, as far as the world at large tells us. Often enough, when I walked into a treatment room, I could see in my patients' eyes that I wasn't whom they were expecting.

I recall one incident in particular that involved a patient who needed surgery for heavy uterine bleeding. I walked into the pre-op room with my white coat on and introduced myself as Dr. Semien. The expressions on the faces of her family members were anxious and confused. In a tone that was part inquiry and part disbelief, one of her family members blurted out, "Are you the doctor?" I felt that question doubly hard because I had already introduced myself as the physician who would be taking care of their family member. Yes, I was young, but I also felt the question was linked to the color of my skin.

Despite the pit in my stomach, I remained professional. I explained the procedure and its risks and benefits to the family. Afterward, I returned to my office to pray, just as I always did before operating. I was deeply saddened by their prejudice. My mind began swimming. Even though this was a fairly routine surgery, I considered consulting with my partner because I didn't feel that the family trusted me with their loved one. I was badly shaken and felt myself at a disadvantage—if the surgery was not a complete success, I worried that the family would sue for malpractice. Nonetheless, I knew I was the right doctor to help this woman—even if her family did not.

The surgery went smoothly. After washing up, I went to the waiting room to report to the family. To my surprise, the room was packed with twenty more relatives. When I told them the surgery was a success, their relief was priceless. Whether or not the bluntness of the offending question had more to do with the family's anxiety, I will never truly know.

Today, I have the privilege of caring for several generations of that family. I believe in my heart that everything happens for a reason and that, as my mother always taught me, a large percentage of the time, we need to just sit silently and wait for God's message to unfold. Sometimes stress and fear cause us to be less than our best selves. Being black is often an added burden. You are always having to second-guess every interaction to determine if someone treated you badly because of your race or if it had nothing to do with your race at all. This is a burden that I had to just learn to accept.

In those first months of practice, I became more and more blessed. When I had arrived in Lake Charles, I knew absolutely no one, but the longer I was at the practice, the more people entered my life; they all offered me support in ways I never could have anticipated. In particular, Mrs. Tammy, our nurse practitioner, and Mrs. Nolia, our medical records administrator, were willing to give 110 percent to lift me up. Not only were they willing to help me with anything I needed on a daily basis, but they both also knew the community very well and spoke highly of me to their friends and family. They helped me to connect to my new community, which helped me build a rapport with my patients. Through both their words and deeds, they showed me how much they cared about my family and me as we started our new life in Lake Charles.

My patient list grew rapidly, and unfortunately, without meaning to, I believe I got a bit overconfident. I was humbled quickly when my partner got sick, because it was up to me to run the entire practice. I had to balance caring for her established patient roster while also tending to those on my growing list of patients. The stress was overwhelming. Some days, I didn't know if I was coming or going.

God humbled me, but once I remembered Him and brought Him back to the center of my life, He blessed me yet again. He brought me the support of the staff and other doctors, and soon a new physician joined the practice. With fewer demands and less stress at work, I was once again able to spend quality time with my wife and children.

A few months later, I began preparing for my very last test: the oral board exam. On the one hand, my practice was still growing, but on the other hand, I knew gaining this last certification was crucial to my career. I could not put it off. Even though studying meant sacrificing more time with my family, I gave prep my all. I worked with other physicians who were also preparing for the oral board, and we would study together late into the night.

The oral board exam is different from all other tests. Conducted by a panel of certified ob-gyns, the exam is somewhere in between a conversation and an interrogation. I was confident in my knowledge, skills, and patient care, but I remembered all the times as a child when I stuttered or just plain couldn't get my words out. The fear lurking inside me made the oral board the most stressful test I ever had to face.

When exam day came, I believe I was more nervous than I had ever been in my life. Now I would have to prove to established doctors that I was truly one of their peers. I had to be able to vocally express that I was a competent, caring, fully trained ob-gyn. The exam lasted six long, tense hours. As I left the testing room, I thought receiving my grade would feel tiny next to the relief of having completed the exam.

As it turned out, the hardest part of my oral exam was not the prep, nor the test, nor my anxieties. The most difficult thing was waiting for the results, which took a full week. What bothered me more than anything was trying to figure out what I would say to my twelve- and seven-year-old sons if I failed. As parents, my wife and I had always stressed that hard work and true dedication are the equivalent of success. Our sons earned good grades in school not because grades were important, but because we taught them that the effort was important. Yet in the adult world, things are much more complex. All the effort in the world and all the little league games I had missed wouldn't matter one bit if I didn't pass. How would I explain this to my sons? Plus, the thought of doing all that studying again, and missing even more time with my sons, was frightening.

My anxieties proved to be misplaced. The best days had finally come. By passing the oral exam, I was officially a board-certified ob-gyn. My decade and a half of work had now borne its sweetest fruits. After I completed my boards, my practice continued to grow, and it is still flourishing to this day. May these humble doctor's hands of mine always be guided by His blessings.

My responsibilities do not end with being a doctor and a father. As a black man, I have a duty to my community and an obligation to speak to all young people of color. Any young person from a minority community who has big dreams and even bigger ambitions needs to know that, yes, there is a path to success.

My next step is to begin speaking to minority youth about the lack of black doctors practicing medicine today. There are many reasons for the lack of black doctors—income disparity, subpar schools, racial bias—but above all else, I believe it's because young people of color across the board are not expected to succeed and are therefore afraid to even try. Fear of failure haunts us all, but especially for those of African descent, it's not failure itself that counts; it's how we respond to failure that makes the difference. No one's journey in life is perfect; my own life is a testament to that.

The adage, "If you don't try, you'll never succeed" is true, but that's only half the story. You can't succeed if you let failure, or fear of it, stop you. Had I failed my oral board exam, for example, I would have tried again—if for no other reason than to be a role model for my sons. As I begin my advocacy work with young people of color, I want them to understand one thing first and foremost: with God's guidance, there is no challenge too great, no failure too crushing, and no goal that cannot be achieved with determination and perseverance.

AFTERWORD

By Dr. Norman C. Francis, President Emeritus, Xavier University of Louisiana

FORTY YEARS AGO, WHEN I accepted the presidency of Xavier University of Louisiana, a historically black college in New Orleans, a report came across my desk with a shocking statistic. Even as the nation was starting to realize significant gains from the Civil Rights Movement, the already miniscule number of black physicians was dropping.

As a black man who fought to earn his law degree in the Jim Crow South, I knew that the dearth of black doctors was not due to a lack of intellect among black students nor a lack of desire, but that it was because so many black children remained in separate but unequal schools that left them unable to imagine themselves as doctors and utterly unprepared to pursue medicine as a career.

I also knew as the president of a college whose mission was to serve black students that I was in a unique position to aggressively address with colleagues this alarming trend. And so I dedicated my nearly 50-year tenure as president of Xavier to building an institution that has helped thousands of black students like Pierre Johnson, Maxime Madhere and Joseph Semien, live up to their potential and realize their dreams of becoming physicians.

Our Founder, St. Katharine Drexel started a College of Arts and Sciences in 1925 and added an accredited College of Pharmacy in 1935. Xavier was one of only two colleges of pharmacy in the country and by the time the report came across my desk, the university had a 43-year track record of producing black science, technology and math graduates. My faculty, led by a visionary scientist named Dr. J.W. Carmichael, insisted to me that Xavier could address this healthcare challenge if we revolutionized the way we taught science to underprepared students like Pierre, Max and Joe, but also how we supported them academically and socially. Instead of working to weed out students, Xavier was determined to pull the best out of these students and usher them to success.

Pulse of Perseverance is the embodiment of my dream. This critical book speaks to what can be achieved when instead of squandering the talents of our most disadvantaged youth, we make the decision to nurture them.

That's why I believe that *Pulse of Perseverance* should be read by children across this country no matter their race. This book shows that humble beginnings do not have to constrain your life, and that even when you have setbacks, success can be achieved despite the odds.

This book should also be read by every educator in the country, both in K-12 and college, because far too many of them do not believe that every black and brown child can learn and so they give up on our children far too early. Through their personal stories of failure and triumph, Pierre, Max and Joe demonstrate what can be achieved when every student is pushed to the limits of their academic potential, and in doing so, these doctors provide a clarion call to teachers across the country.

I am proud of these young men, but there is still so much work to do. Despite tiny, little Xavier producing more black doctors than any other institution, fewer black men became doctors in 2015 than they did in 1978. This is a national failure and a national shame and so the lessons in *Pulse of Perseverance* are needed now more than ever.

Pulse of Perseverance shines a spotlight on the problem. But much more than that, it provides a roadmap for the solution, if only we are willing to listen.

GLOSSARY: COMMONLY USED TERMS AND ACRONYMS

Attendings:

Attendings are staff physicians at a hospital or similar facility who have primary responsibility for the treatment of patients in a given department or ward. Attendings supervise the care patients receive from senior medical students, interns, residents, and fellows.

Board Exams/Certification:

After the completion of at least three residency years, the American Board of Medical Specialists certifies physicians in their area of expertise through a series of specialty-specific tests. Board certification is voluntary but demonstrates a physician's high level of expertise in a particular specialty or subspecialty. Physicians must keep their certification current by periodically participating in Maintenance of Certification programs. Patients who choose board-certified doctors can be confident that their physicians have met all criteria for the highest standards of care.

Clerkships:

Also called rotations. Medical students who have completed two years of medical school and who have passed all required exams serve in unpaid work-study positions where they rotate through different medical specialties (internal medicine, general surgery, pediatrics, etc.) in order to gain clinical experience and an introduction to medicine's many specialty areas.

Clerkship programs are two years long and are the bulk of a medical student's last two years of school. Clerkships are closely supervised, and students must pass an exit exam at the end of each specialty rotation.

HBCUs:

Historically black colleges and universities; HBCUs are institutions of higher education in the United States that have the primary mission of providing postsecondary education to black and African American students (although HBCUs are open to students of all races). All HBCUs were founded prior to 1964, and there are over one hundred HBCUs, both public and private, in existence today. Xavier University of Louisiana, which all three of this book's authors attended, is the only Catholic HBCU in the nation.

Interns:

Interns are first-year medical residents. See *residency*.

Match day/match system:

The National Resident Matching Program facilitates the placement of matriculating medical students into available residencies at US teaching hospitals. Fourth-year medical students interview with possible residency programs; then interviewers rank residency candidates, and candidates rank residency preferences. A computer system matches interviewees with residency programs. Once all available positions in a given program are filled, the residency is closed to further applications. This makes many residency slots highly competitive.

MCAT:

Medical College Admission Test; developed and administered by the Association of American Medical Colleges, the MCAT is a standardized, multiple-choice exam created to help medical schools assess applicants' problem-solving skills, critical thinking abilities, and knowledge of various life-science concepts. Passing the MCAT is required for admission into the vast majority of American medical schools. Medical schools outside the United States, such as Saint Matthew's University (which coauthor Joe Semien attended), often take a whole-applicant approach to admissions, and therefore an MCAT score is not required.

MD:

Medical degree; a medical degree is conferred after an individual has completed four years of medical school and successfully passed both the USMLE Step 1 and USMLE Step 2. Those who hold an MD have a restricted license to practice medicine.

MEDPREP:

The Medical/Dental Education Preparatory Program at Southern Illinois University's School of Medicine; established in 1972, MEDPREP is a graduate-level program designed to provide assistance to educationally and/or economically disadvantaged baccalaureate-holding students, thereby preparing them to achieve success in the health professions. Two of this book's authors, Max Madhere and Pierre Johnson, attended MEDPREP's one-year Traditional Program to strengthen their MCAT scores before moving on to medical school. For students who continue on to a second year of study, MEDPREP offers master's degrees in both public health and biological science.

Residency/residents:

Residency is a stage of medical training during which newly licensed physicians serve on the staff of a teaching hospital and provide direct patient care, although this care is always under the supervision of attendings or other senior staff. Depending on the area of specialization, residency programs range from three to seven years; first-year residents are called interns. Whereas medical school's two clerkship years teach a broad range of knowledge along with basic clinical skills, residents receive in-depth training within a specific area of medicine.

Rotations:

Medical students who have completed two years of medical school, and who have passed all requisite exams, serve in unpaid work-study positions where they rotate through medical specialties. See *clerkships*.

USMLE Step 1, Step 2, and Step 3:

The United States Medical Licensing Exam; the USMLE is an exam in three parts, which medical students and intern-level residents must pass as they advance toward unrestricted licensure.

- The USMLE Step 1 is the first exam, which is taken at the end of medical school's second year. Students who do not pass the USMLE Step 1 are not allowed to advance into clerkships.
- The USMLE Step 2 is taken in the fourth year of medical school and is a requirement for the conference of a medical degree and restricted medical licensure.
- The USMLE Step 3 is most often taken at the end of a resident's intern year. Without passing the USMLE Step 3, a physician cannot pursue further specialty training or board certification.

THE AUTHORS

PICTURED ABOVE, FROM LEFT TO right:

Dr. Maxime Madhere: Diplomate of the American Board of Anesthesiology
Diplomate of the National Board of Echocardiography

Dr. Pierre Johnson: Fellow, American Congress of Obstetricians and Gynecologists

Dr. Joseph Semien Jr.: Fellow, American Congress of Obstetricians and Gynecologists

www.thepulseofp3.com

CPSIA information can be obtained
at www.ICGtesting.com
Printed in the USA
LVHW041421170319
610892LV00001B/26